BEHIND EVERY GREAT WOMAN
THERE'S A FABULOUS GAY MAN

BEHIND EVERY GREAT WOMAN

There's a

Fabulous Gay Man

Advice from a Guy
Who Gives It to You Straight

DAVE SINGLETON

A PERIGEE BOOK

A Perigee Book
Published by the Penguin Group
Penguin Group (USA) Inc.
375 Hudson Street, New York, New York 10014, USA
Penguin Group (Canada), 10 Alcorn Avenue, Toronto, Ontario M4V 3B2, Canada
(a division of Pearson Penguin Canada Inc.)
Penguin Books Ltd., 80 Strand, London WC2R 0RL, England
Penguin Group Ireland, 25 St. Stephen's Green, Dublin 2, Ireland (a division of Penguin Books Ltd.)
Penguin Group (Australia), 250 Camberwell Road, Camberwell, Victoria 3124, Australia
(a division of Pearson Australia Group Pty. Ltd.)
Penguin Books India Pvt. Ltd., 11 Community Centre, Panchsheel Park, New Delhi - 110 017, India
Penguin Group (NZ), cnr Airborne and Rosedale Roads, Albany, Auckland 1310, New Zealand
(a division of Pearson New Zealand Ltd.)
Penguin Books (South Africa) (Pty.) Ltd., 24 Sturdee Avenue, Rosebank, Johannesburg 2196, South Africa

Penguin Books Ltd., Registered Offices: 80 Strand, London WC2R 0RL, England

PRINTING HISTORY
Perigee trade paperback edition / April 2005

PERIGEE is a registered trademark of Penguin Group (USA) Inc.
The "P" design is a trademark belonging to Penguin Group (USA) Inc.

Library of Congress Cataloging-in-Publication Information
Singleton, Dave, 1961–
    Behind every great woman there's a fabulous gay man / Dave Singleton.—1st Perigee pbk. ed.
        p. cm.
    ISBN 0-399-53082-7
    1. Gay men—Relations with heterosexual women. 2. Single women—Psychology. 3. Single
women—Life skills guides. 4. Dating (Social customs) 5. Man-woman relationships. I. Title.

HQ76.S55 2005
306.7—dc22   2004055097

PRINTED IN THE UNITED STATES OF AMERICA

10 9 8 7 6 5 4 3 2 1

To the fabulous women behind this very grateful man.
To Elizabeth, who came first.

ACKNOWLEDGMENTS

Behind this gay man are the smartest, coolest, sexiest, deepest, funniest, brilliant, and, yes, *fabulous,* women in the world. To borrow a line from Oprah's magazine column, this is *what I know for sure.*

There's no way that this book (or most of the good things in my life) would have happened without the incredible women who inspired it—namely, Ava Seave, Carol Levine, Lucille Santarelli, Rachel Kahan, Cara Carroccia, Tracy Cisek, Lisa Malmud, Sonya Clark, Kristy Darcey, Madeline Dolente, Sarah Brezniak, Margaret Rosen, Laura Ribas, Susan Strawbridge, Liz Wilson, Karen Quinn, Liz Sorota, Dia Black, Linda Dickey, Marcie Rosenstock, Brenda Councill, Sharon Hubley, Rose Fiorilli, Dori Sless, and Suzanne Rittereiser. For the inspiration and support of this book above and beyond the call of duty, thanks to Bonnie Maglio,

Cathy Alter, Cathleen Rittereiser, Carol Nicotera-Ward, Christina Rudolf, Andrea Sims, Melissa Fireman, Abby Wilner, Bobbi Whalen, Mary Ann Voight, Amy Gussack, Stacy Chavis, and Jamie Levine. This is, at heart, a book about an essential, agendaless friendship, and I know something about that thanks to them.

A very special thanks to "my best girl" Jan, and to the fantastic women in my family: Elizabeth, Amy, Judi, Kaya, Katie, Libby, Lee, and Jennifer.

How do I thank the hundred and eleven women from around the country who participated in my research for this book? From late-night phone calls to stark Starbucks confessionals while inquiring minds listened in, to martinis in swank bars, I loved hearing your stories more than you know. I am not sure what was more eye-opening: interviewing women I'd never met, or learning things I didn't know about my close friends.

Thanks also to:

The other gay boyfriends who shared their stories with me.

My straight guy friends, brothers, and nephew who are part of a new, better, less uptight world where gay and straight men are friends like we should be. And remember, I don't care what you do in private, please just don't flaunt yourselves. All that hand-holding and kissing your wives and girlfriends in public. *Please*.

Shane Harris, Bill McGinn, Bruce Morman, James Hollander, Aron Wilson, Peter Pappas, Steve Kempf, Kevin Mischka, Russell Schrader, Tom Downing, Michael Privitera, Matt Wehland, Joe Lynch, Scott Henrichsen, Manny and Lee Lemas, Jim Hall, and Jim Horner.

Darren, Chuck, Amy, Laura, Bill, Leslie, Maureen, Jamie, Tom, Lea, and Gretchen at "The B."

Bruce Shenitz, Lori Draper, Sonya Castex, my prolific, witty, and wise writer's group, and the editors and publishers who've supported my work, and taught me much.

The wonderful crew at Perigee Books, including Christel Winkler, who joined this ship midcruise, kept us on course, and got the book and me to harbor safely! Thank you for being such a personal and professional joy. Thanks also to: Craig Burke and Tess Tabor for their enthusiasm and promotional support, Ben Gibson who designed the groovy cover, managing editor Kim Koren, and everyone who helped this book get into the right hands. A very special thanks to Katie McHugh, who was a cheerleader for this book. Thanks for your early support and insights, Katie!

My awesome agent, Paula Balzer, who's savvy, smart, and fun, as well as Sarah Lazin and Catherine Mayhew for your support.

My partner Vic for inspiring me with his relentless (and sometimes exhausting) drive to turn off bad TV, knock back the Red Bulls, and make dreams like this book come true.

CONTENTS

WHY EVERY GIRL NEEDS A GAY
BOYFRIEND

Not all gay men give good advice. I know it's shocking, especially to a smart, urbane girl who chooses her gay men well. But it's true. Good gay advice is not something you can count on 100 percent, like death, your one "horror-show" boyfriend, and PMS.

Though it's not 100 percent foolproof, it's pretty damn close. I should know.

I first realized the power behind a gay man giving a woman good advice about twenty years ago, when I was just a "wee gay," barely out and just graduated from college in Virginia, a state not known for its prominent fags. My best friend at the time, Cara, was having a man crisis. Back then, a man crisis meant you were crazy about a man who didn't know you existed. Now, a man crisis means he knows you exist, and so does the judge who gave you the restraining order and full custody of the kids. Or maybe your man crises have evolved from college girl crushes to full blown fatal attractions. Instead of a warm pat on the shoulder, I need to stop you from calling his wife, boiling his bunny, and blowing the lid off of your latest inappropriate affair with another married man. You've come a long way, baby. Yes, your crises may be bigger, but then again, it's all relative, isn't it?

Cara, who normally let her red hair cascade around her face in flattering, flirtatious waves, now sat at the kitchen table with her do pulled back into two pigtails. She looked more like Pippi Longstocking's bipolar older sister than the hot babe she was. For the first time, I grasped that hairstyle is a leading indicator of a girl's mood, which in this case was severely depressed. She was minutes away from both her graduate degree in architecture and a meltdown, sitting at home on a Saturday night, crying, morose, and drinking the last of my Wild Turkey. Why? Because the guy we called "Marriageable Mike," the sort of hot-looking idiot who peaks at twenty and is miserable in a minivan somewhere dull right now, told her he wasn't interested in a commitment. On the surface, it might have seemed obvious that a graduating senior would have his sights set on life beyond school. But if I learned anything from my own life, it's that one man's melodrama is another man's drama. In other words, the circumstances didn't matter. Cara's feelings mattered. I listened, I hugged, I boosted her confidence, and I totally shot down Marriageable Mike. I wasn't sure what to do, so I mentioned going out for a drink. Her eyes lit up. After sliding her into her black miniskirt and slathering her eyes in raccoon eye makeup until she looked like "The

Rose," we left home for a pub crawl. Finally, at 2 a.m., I left her doing cartwheels in the parking lot next to TJ's bar surrounded by men. "She got some eyes on her," as they say in the South. Meaning, she got what she needed: a little attention from the opposite sex.

On that auspicious night, a new gay best friend was born, and another gay angel got his wings. Next thing I knew, I'd become one part muse, one part best friend, and one part gay Dr. Phil.

WHAT DOES THE GAY BOYFRIEND BRING TO YOUR PARTY?

From advice about clothes (I hate to give it, but apparently I am good at it) to getting at least three women emotionally sober enough to say, "I do," I have been on call for two decades. Who am I in your life? I am the guy who sees the real you. I am the one who comes running to your house when you're panicked about a first date. I see the crazy, hysterical person, hanging together with glue and a bobby pin, predate. But within an hour, you're walking into the restaurant to meet Mr. Maybe and exuding an air of cool confidence. Is this sea of change something that happens without the magic of me, your gay godfather? I don't think so.

I've sat with you at Starbucks dissecting more "smart women, foolish choices" than Oprah, Dr. Phil, and Carrie Bradshaw combined. I've heard about how you see your mother's hidden agenda but no one else can (that old chestnut) so many times that I literally hold my eyes in place to keep them from rolling out of my head and down the street.

Do I keep my mouth shut and just listen? No, of course I don't. That's not my job. I am not your dad. Like me, Dad has a unique place in your life, but you can't tell him everything, now can you? While Dad might be shocked by some of your secrets, I consider it my duty to calmly consider all the messy details of your latest crisis. I am not your girlfriend. Your girlfriend is like a hurricane, powerful but volatile. She's the one you relate to, fight with, and then skip down the street like sisters with, your hands entwined in search of ice cream and a manicure. I am not your brother. We all know he's got too many issues and family dynamics at stake to lay it all on the line. One misstatement out of him and you'll "knock his block off," like Lucy did to Linus in the *Peanuts* comic strip. (I readily admit that, even in my own family, the brother card trumps the gay boyfriend card. I am sure my sister wishes she could tap into all the sound gay boyfriend advice that other women in my life get with no familial agenda.) I am not your boyfriend, either. As if you'd ever ask him for advice anyway, the lunk. But still, you love him. Ah, love. It's blind, deaf, and dumb at times.

No, I am in a class all by myself.

I've spent the last twenty years giving increasingly complicated advice to smart, funny, and beautiful women who sometimes should know better but never fail to call. They know I will give them the guidance and support that no one else in their lives can give them. I am not just the run-of-the-mill gay pal. That kind of gay friend is a dime a dozen at this point in history. No, I am "gay best friend on steroids," the gay boyfriend who pumps you up when you get emotionally deflated, helps you up when you fall, and lifts you up to new heights that you might not reach on your own. It doesn't matter if you are single or coupled. Having a gay boyfriend is essential to your emotional well-being. Even if your real boyfriend gets a little jealous, he still can't object. After all, as *Sex and the City* stated so clearly: "Gay boyfriends are the loophole of monogamy." You can't get the kind of advice I give you, the way I give it to you, from anyone else. That kind of advice is what I want to share with you in *Behind Every Great Woman, There's a Fabulous Gay Man*.

WHY DO I DO IT? BECAUSE IT'S MY JOB

Everyone knows by now that there's an unusually strong bond between gay men and straight women. That's not news. There's Rock and Doris from the closeted years. Will and Grace on television. Rupert and Julia at the movies in *My Best Friend's Wedding*. Gay men and straight women have become a classic, archetypal couple. In some ways, it's a relationship born of shared interests: style, the Oscars, decorating, clothes, working out, music, and martinis, to name a few. And let's not leave out men. Okay, and some of us can be a little dramatic as well, which you appreciate.

That's the stereotype, and let's face it. Stereotypes are often based on at least some truth. But the reality goes way beyond that. Many straight women consider gay guys their closest confidants, confessors, and advisors. By my rough calculations, I've given counsel to more than three hundred women in a relatively short period of time. I have gotten so good at what I do that it's like breathing to me now. Just last week, my days began and ended with offering sage advice to women. My schedule looked something like this:

Gay Boyfriend Weekly Schedule

MONDAY: Help Carrie save her marriage. She's being insecure and is about to lose the best thing that's happened to her since she cut back on carbs. Her husband is not the problem, she is. So explain Male 101 behavior to her in a voice she'll understand. Now is no time to hold back. Tell her she can either continue to be a "black hole of emotional need" or she can grow up.

TUESDAY: Stop Angie from getting married since she hasn't figured out on her own yet that Fiancé Phil is a philandering idiot. To paraphrase an old proverb, "There are none so blind as those who will not see." Insist that she replace her current motto ("Better living through denial") with a new one ("I will not get married with my eyes closed").

WEDNESDAY: Get Sarah over her guilt for having an office fling with the hot idiot who fixes computers. It's been two years since she's had a real date, and, until the sky opens up, angels sing and it starts raining men, she needs something to get her through another quiet Saturday night. Get her to accept the concept of a "transitional man" so that she won't confuse him with a long-term boyfriend.

THURSDAY: Talk Karen down from the ledge after Jewish singles night at temple. Explain to her once more that the odds are not in her favor at events like this. Why? It's simple. Do the math. Once a month, thirty sexy women vie for the attention of four nerdy male accountants who cannot believe their luck. Talk about casting pearls before swine! At best, it's bad odds. It's like me looking for love at a gay circuit party full of the hottest men on the planet. Help her find new and better options for unearthing dates. If ever a mitzvah was called for, this is it.

FRIDAY: Spend the day transforming Linda's apartment, once a haven for mangy cats and old magazines, into a swinging bachelorette pad. Start by 8 a.m., since she has a date arriving at 7 p.m. Buy martini glasses for her to add a little sophistication. Once you have them in hand, make sure to down a couple of appletinis before executing the stuffed animals mafia-style and shredding the age-inappropriate Hello Kitty sheets in her frilly bedroom. Yuck! This is a dirty job but someone has to do it.

SATURDAY: Start the day bright and early the morning of Lisa's wedding, as I prep to be Bridesman of Honor at the 5 p.m. ceremony. I must wear several hats today, including "empathetic best friend," "fearless Bridezilla handler," and "supervisor of the incompetent and overpaid wedding director." In the morning, be stern yet loving as I comfort Lisa with one arm and use the other to knock the Krispy Kreme doughnuts out of her hand so she'll fit in her dress. In the afternoon, finalize music selections so that there will be no "Macarena" at the reception. And two hours before the ceremony, don my cleric outfit to hear her weepy last "sex and the single girl" confession before pushing her down the aisle and into the arms of the man I lovingly refer to as "My Second in Command."

SUNDAY: Rest.

OUR RELATIONSHIP GOES BEYOND THE STEREOTYPE

Remember Roseanne's remark a few years ago in her standup act that, "Without gay men, who would dance with all us fat women?" We're well beyond that old cliché now. We're beyond codependence. We're beyond fag-hags and stereotypes like the overprotective sister to the wild gay boy, the gay male nanny to immature girls, and the scared twosome who cling to each other to avoid intimacy with real partners. The truth these days is more expansive, cutting across the really important areas of life such as love, style, fashion, and self-esteem. The truth today is more like, "Without gay men, who's going to make sure you don't end up marrying a loser, spending all your money on crappy home decor, looking like a reject from a bad 80s hair band, and spending the next fifty years entrenched in the core belief that losing those last five pounds will really change your life?"

I tell you things that no one else does. And though I am

sometimes brutally honest, it's not so bad hearing it when it comes from me, is it? What are some of the things I tell you? That outfit isn't working. Do not give him a third chance. Your biological clock went off two years ago and apparently you weren't listening. Get off the StairMaster and lift some weights so your upper arms won't jiggle like grandma's do. Frilly curtains, flowery patterns on anything, writing on *Lizzie McGuire* stationery, and more than three teddy bears on your bed after the age of twenty-five are sexual turnoffs.

Why do I do this? It's not just that I love you (I do). It's that gay guys are born observers. We have to be to survive in a world where we know we're different. Because of this, many of us develop a good eye for people, fashion, and style, along with an ability to cut through directly to the heart of what matters most to you.

I'd never purport that gay men are only one-dimensional stereotypes. We know that's not true. Ignoring the whole person is a surefire way to marginalize him, and our lives are too complicated to ever be one-dimensional. Finally, we're seeing a return to the approach that traits somehow thought of as "gay" in our culture now—treating ourselves better, attention to detail in everything from cooking to home design, striving for excellence, matching the external to the internal—are, in fact, just "good" traits.

GAY OR STRAIGHT, MEN ARE MEN

When it comes to men, who better than me to give you glimpses into the rarefied world of how men really think? As twenty-six-year-old Shane points out, "Gay men make perfect counselors for beleaguered straight chicks. That's because in addition to having the sex drive, biology, and socialization of men, we also have the sensitivity of women. We can commiserate, because we know men are pigs. But we're also guys, and can give them insights that their girlfriends, for reasons of basic biology, cannot. Gay men give women the best advice about men for a very simple reason: gay men know exactly how straight men think. We know precisely what straight men are trying to do with women. We can tell our straight girlfriends this with impunity, too, because we're certainly not trying to get into the sack with them, and therefore have nothing to lose."

Plus, gay and straight men like the same things, too: making money, sex, toys (not necessarily together in the same sentence), and focusing on work. We're both fiercely competitive and aggressive.

So think of it as getting a bird's-eye view into what might at times seem like a mysterious male world. Or, as Cathleen puts it, our bird's-eye view gives us "street cred." "You have the perspective of a guy, but a different sensibility, too."

In the last few years, gay men have negotiated a much healthier, easier relationship with straight men. To borrow from the old cliché, some of my closest friends are straight men. Their attitude with me seems to be "It doesn't affect me, dude. People are people. If two guys want to sleep together, that just frees up two women for the rest of us. Works for me."

A gay man telling the truth about his perceptions works in their favor, too. We do not hop on the bandwagon of "everything straight men do is wrong," because that's a load of crap. I am a friend and sometimes even a conduit to introductions. Sometimes I can even make a good match between my straight male and female friends. I know that my ladies trust my judgment. But finally, the straight men are learning that when I say, "the girl is hot," I know what I am talking about. As I told my straight friend Peter, "I am gay, not blind," after I weaseled out of him the real reason he was turning down the fix-up with stunning Liz. The real reason was that he thought when I said she was a hot, thirty-two-year-old, light-blond, gorgeous marketing executive, he somehow translated that into "she's got a great personality." He soon found out how wrong his first impression was and another stereotype went up in shrapnel.

With *Queer Eye for the Straight Guy* on television about twenty times a week, straight-gay friendships between men have lost their taboo. Straight men like having the gays around. We are entertaining and make straight men feel better about just being themselves. Gay men like having their straight guy friends, or "fag stags," as we call them. It might come as a surprise to some, but gay guys need a break from gay guys. Being gay among gays is a lot of pressure. Plus, we definitely like busting each other's chops.

THE MAN WITH NO AGENDA, THAT'S ME

Shane makes a good point about lack of agenda. The dynamics between gay men and straight women are about as pure as you get. Doesn't it sometimes seem as if everyone in your life has an agenda? That's why, for better or worse, I am the one man in your life who always gives it to you straight. Oh sure, I've got an agenda sometimes. But none tied to you. You don't have to be the perfect daughter, sister, girlfriend, or wife with me. In many cases, we have less of an agenda than other men in your life. As my friend Roberta says, "There's a push toward wanting something specific to happen, to make me do something in a specific way. They want an outcome. My brother and father want me to find a guy and get married. My father just doesn't get that I like my single life, that it affords me great joy and happiness. My life has very little value for them, as I stand now as a single woman, not being taken care of by a man."

It helps that we're not in any sort of "girl" competition over status, looks, or popularity.

Despite our many similarities, there are differences, which means I bring a different perspective than the girls.

As Paula, twenty-nine-year-old literary agent in New York, says, "In my late twenties, I found myself inundated by advice from girlfriends. But the truth is, they were reinforcing all my bad decisions. In retrospect, I see that they were all in the same boat as me. My gay friends were the ones willing to call me on the carpet. 'You need to get accountable,' one of them said to me at a time when my girlfriends actually thought they were being helpful by just offering sympathy."

As a gay man, I can relate to this. There are times in all of our lives when we reach out extensively to others for feedback on day-to-day drama. I remember my late twenties, single in New York City, when I didn't go to the subway without asking a team of people for their opinions. Like Paula's girlfriends, my gay guy friends were in the same boat as me, yet I sought their opinions on everything from career to my bad dating choices. There were times when only my girlfriends were able to help me "get accountable." There are advantages to having what my friend Cathleen calls a "personal advisory board," as long as you will get more than just one-note feedback. But when people around you are all in the same boat, their advice is often merely "collective insanity."

Or, as in the case of Amy, a twenty-one-year-old college student, "Some girls don't tell you the truth because they don't want to hurt your feelings. That's a noble intent, but not always helpful. Gay guys just seem so much more impatient with bullshit. I think it's because that, in order to feel accepted, they've had to sugarcoat so much of their lives when they are closeted, and they are just tired of it. That, and the fact that so much of the gay scene is b.s., their b.s. detectors are strong."

And for gay men and straight women of color, the bond goes even deeper. "Within black-queer relationships, you have the chance to deal with the specific hardships of race," says Greer, twenty-three-year-old in Washington, D.C. "Black gay men and black straight women have an extra level of bonding."

Finally, with the exception of an occasional bisexual, we won't be after the same man (after all, isn't finding a true bisexual man an occasion, kind of like discovering a white tiger?). I promise you that if that situation ever comes up, you can have him if you want him. But be forewarned: my overprotective gene will kick in and I'll probably advise you to quit wasting your time with him and "get accountable" about that, too.

FOR BETTER OR WORSE, YOUR GAY BOYFRIEND HAS YOUR BACK

Perhaps most importantly, when I've committed to being your gay best friend, no one is as fiercely loyal to you. Maybe there's a certain kind of fair-weather gay pal who's eager to be friends with whomever he meets. Not me. I pick and choose much more carefully than some might think. You're either all in or all out. As Cher recently said, "Gay men are so loyal to you; I mean, people can just bash you and dis you, but if gay men love you, they love you, and they don't really leave you. The thing is, gay men either love you or they don't even take into account your existence."

WISDOM BORN OF EXPERIENCE

This book is not just *Will & Grace* in book form. It is Will giving advice based on the life lessons he's learned from the many Graces in his life. Where else are you going to find advice that cuts across so many important areas? I am your handyman, man Friday, counselor, and a guy for all seasons, multifaceted enough to segue from relationship advice to workout tips to home improvement in a single afternoon.

For example, you can finally face your fears of home decoration with someone who'll help you fix the problems, not judge you. Your friends and family may think you're confident when it comes to choosing paint color and buying furniture, but I know the truth. You are terrified. And no amount of advice from *Martha Stewart Living* can help when rubber meets the road and you are forced to pull out the credit card at Pottery Barn. That's when I become your personal shopper and home designer to help you sort out the best options before you waste your time and money.

With me, you can safely confront the "ten pound" myth. Is losing ten pounds going to drastically change your life? No. That doesn't mean you can't have those bonding times with your girlfriends at the gym, gossiping on side-by-side treadmills as you work up enough of a sweat to make you feel deserving of an occasional chocolate dessert. But my book will take on the real issue behind this perpetual weight loss scheme, which has, over time, become your personal search for the Holy Grail.

And when it comes to dating, *Behind Every Great Woman, There's a Fabulous Gay Man* will do what any gay best friend worth his salt would do. It'll stop you from letting your inner lunatic out in front of him before he's had a chance to fall madly, hopelessly, and eternally in love with you. For example, I'll point out the differences between postdate stalking behaviors, such as two page e-mails sent to the poor lug at his office the morning after, and a healthy slow burn. Even typically smart, busy, and insightful women sometimes devolve into clingy, insecure, lost souls before, during, and after dates. If this kind of deevolution is a habit, you don't need advice from your mother. She either wants you to get married or be safe and stay inside. Can your girlfriends really help when they're in the same screwed-up boat, want to shower you with a warm blanket of compassion, or maybe judge you a little too harshly? No. You need a linear thinker at this point to guide you. Not the beer-swilling, I-like-sports-bars-and-Pamela-Anderson type of linear thinker. You need a linear thinker who equates getting over breakups with buying a new pair of Jimmy Choo pumps.

THE UNSPOKEN BROTHER/SISTERHOOD

The point is this: you are not alone! If, like Cara, you've been sitting at your own kitchen table, drinking someone else's booze, feeling morose and wondering what to do, now you'll have the answers in black and white.

Of course, there can be some downsides to the gay best friend relationship. Sometimes there's an unresolved crush on the boy who can't reciprocate in a romantic way. As Roberta says, "With every other male friend you have, there's always the possibility, a thin wire of sexual tension that's there. There's something interesting and exclusionary about that. Getting out of the shower on a cruise with gay guys, there was a part of me that kept thinking that "Hey, they should be looking, they should at least be turning around." Sometimes, the gay man feels love for a beautiful, smart, funny woman that seems so much more uncompli-cated and fulfilling than trying to find happiness in the often tough gay world. I know that's been true for me. Then there are women and gay men who form romantic attachments to each other, or who use each other to avoid intimacy with others.

Twenty years after that fateful night with Cara, I don't have just one close female friend. I have many. Listening to the stories of women and other gay men, I have since learned that gay boyfriends are everywhere and that my friendship with Cara was typical of many gay boyfriend relationships that often begin when the guy isn't "out" yet. She might have been first, but she wasn't the last.

If you have a gay best friend (the kind who gives it to you straight), I assure you he'll be relieved to have this book's backup support in his noble quest to offer you the sound advice he knows you need. If he doesn't have my wealth of experience or if he can't be with you twenty-four/seven, then keep this book handy.

If you don't, then you don't know what you've been missing. Maybe you've been going through life facing the bumps in the road by seeking advice from competitive girlfriends, your emotionally clueless boyfriend, or worse, your controlling mother. Is it any wonder you still have that vague, unsatisfied feeling? Not to me, it isn't.

Behind Every Great Woman, There's a Fabulous Gay Man will give you the clarity you've been missing from me, the proudly irreplaceable gay man in your life.

IT'S A TWO-WAY STREET

Of course, the awesome women in my life could easily write a book about helping the gay man or men in their lives (and come to think of it, maybe one of you should). Clearly, it's a two-way street. The concept of "tough love" gained recognition in the 1970s for fighting addictions. But it applies to gay men and straight women who honestly and directly tell each other the truth, sometimes painfully and often with great humor, but always with the goal of making a positive difference. When I decided to write this book, I wanted it to be a valentine to the fabulous women in my life, to bring light and laughter to their lives, and to share with others what we've learned together. I can't count the number of things I have learned from my girlfriends or the number of times I've called on them. My relationships with my close female friends are in a league of their own. The category is bigger than friend, steadier than romance, and responsible like family.

Sadly, I have made a lot of the same mistakes that are recounted in this book, especially when it comes to dating and relationships, as anyone who read my book *The Mandates: 25 Real Rules for Successful Gay Dating* would know all too well. But there's nothing more fervent than a convert, right? When you feel like you've learned something, you want to share it.

Of course, being a fix-it type of man who, after listening for years, wants his female friends to shine, the book is full of my advice. As my friend Bonnie says, "I always know you are rooting for me." Though not a gay trait, enthusiasm is something that many gay men have in spades. Maybe that's because we know too well how it feels to be behind the 8-ball and to have someone rooting for us. This book is also full of stories from women, some I've known for years and some I just met as part of interviews for this book, because this is about insights into women's lives from the gay male's perspective. I know that nothing speaks louder than the funny, cautionary, poignant, insightful stories that come straight (so to speak) from the women themselves.

Part One

DATING, MEN, AND RELATIONSHIPS

1

THE REPETITIVE, FATAL DATING FLAW THAT'S RUINING YOUR LOVE LIFE

Not again! Stop crying on my shoulder and let's pinpoint the problem.

"I need to not date right now. I need time to find myself, to heal. Maybe in a year, I'll date again." These were the famous last words of art designer Mary Pat, twenty-eight, who turned inward after a disastrous two-year relationship with Don, the traditional meat-and-potatoes government bureaucrat.

She uttered those words two years ago and, indeed, she hibernated for just short of a year. She avoided dates and straight men in general, visited friends, and caught up on reading. But mostly, she sought counsel from me on an almost daily basis. In other words, she did all the things a girl thinks she's supposed to do after a bad relationship finally ends. Then, after the year of abstinence was up, she reentered the dating market only to meet a man, get involved too soon, and end up with an even worse broken heart. It's as if she stopped driving for a year, stepped behind the wheel of a new car, and drove off a cliff. Abstinence didn't make the heart heal, grow fonder, or any of those tired clichés. Without analyzing and changing her behavior, it just provided an intermission between her bad decisions.

My point is this: avoidance is no cure for bad dating experiences. Delving into yourself, uncovering your bad habits, and fixing them is the cure. Don't avoid driving only to run off a cliff next time you get behind the wheel. Don't spend useless tears crying on my shoulder about the bad dates you keep having. They're just water under the bridge. Instead, let's pinpoint the repetitive, fatal dating flaw that's ruining your love life. This is one area where women can take a lesson from gay men. Sure, we get devastated when promising relationships go bad. But gay men are more likely to pick themselves up and get back on the horse, so to speak. Women are more likely to want to retreat to the safe harbor of home and friends. So learn from us: take time if you need it to recover, but don't stay up in the ivory tower too long.

I have spent many unaccredited years counseling women about their dating experiences. It's rare that I've found a sequence of unrelated disasters. There's usually one trait in particular that sinks the love boat every time. After wading through so many dating disaster stories from girlfriends, I know how to quickly isolate the deadly trait and get women to chart a course of correction before it's too late and they take wrong turns.

MISS OVERLY CRITICAL

Missy, thirty-nine, considers herself a success story. She was married recently and is pregnant with her first child. But her success was hard won. A year ago, she had no dating prospects and a past littered with relationship disasters. She wanted marriage and a baby so badly that her biological clock was sounding regular alarms, and she was totally depressed. For these reasons, I knew I had to immerse her in my crash course on overcoming fatal dating flaws. Typically, the personality flaws we've all had for most of our lives aren't going to disappear overnight. What took years to start might take months or years to stop. But in Missy's case, this wasn't going to be a weekly course. There wasn't time. So we talked daily for two months.

Her fatal dating flaw was practically written on her fair-skinned forehead. She had no trouble meeting good men, but was overly critical of the men she dated. The dates never started out badly. All of her boyfriends started out winners, but within weeks, she'd isolate a specific "deal breaker" trait that each guy exhibited. She was like a character from *Seinfeld*. Remember how Jerry, Elaine, and George were masters at finding nitpicky characteristics to criticize in their dates? So was Missy.

Mark, a successful advertising account executive and triathlete, was crazy about her. After about six weeks of dating, he was practically on call to help her with home repairs, walk her dog when she was out of town, and take her out to great restaurants. He kept a busy schedule of work and training, but always made it clear she was a priority. Yet within a few weeks, she referred to him as "spineless." When she told me this, it was all I could do to not shake her like a rag doll. Someone had to point out how ridiculous her comment was! I knew Mark—he went to our gym and, far from spineless, this guy was a total stud. Though Mark moved on quickly to another girl, Missy seemed to pay particular attention to me when I told her that plenty of women, and men for that matter, had noticed Mark's assets. Yes, it was manipulative of me to do that. But I decided to apply a little trick I learned in the gay world. *Nothing makes a gay man or straight woman appreciate a guy quicker than mentioning how hot others are for him.*

Bill, an independently wealthy entrepreneur, didn't fall all over Missy when they met. But there was mutual interest and they quickly agreed to a dinner date. He was, in her words, "attractive, fun, and mysterious." But he also kept some reserve in the first few weeks. A little reserve in the first few weeks of dating is more than appropriate. It's appealing. Normally, she'd be the first to agree with that. But when he didn't call her for two days after their third date, she dumped him. He was "aloof." I listened to her for a while when she told me this and then said, "If he had called you the day after your date, would you have called him spineless instead of aloof? You aren't giving him a chance."

Charlie was athletic, smart, and funny. But he wasn't obsessed with news coverage 24/7 like she was. No, he limited his news interest to one paper a day and the evening news with Peter Jennings on nights when he made it home by 6:30 p.m. That sounded saner to me than news junkies who live for CNN updates every five minutes. But in Missy's mind, this made him as simple as Forrest Gump. Finally, I lost it.

"You have a problem. It's a big problem, too. You shoot down every guy within range. I don't think it's them. I think it's you."

Saying that never goes over well. But I felt it must be said. My friend said she wanted to be married with kids and yet, as I looked ahead at her future, I saw a pretty empty road. No one else called her on her bad behavior. As far as I could tell, her girlfriends just empathized, her parents didn't want to hear about it, and Missy just chalked up her string of bad dates to a combination of bad Irish luck and "being choosy."

We spent a lot of time talking about Charlie. She doubted her decision and missed him terribly. I kept asking her why she'd dump perfectly good guys until she finally realized that she was scared to death she'd end up getting hurt by one of them. It was so obvious, but the obvious problems are sometimes the hardest to really fix. One day, about four weeks after she dumped him, she called to see if he'd be interested in lunch. He declined. He didn't want to talk with her. She called him several more times, each time owning up more and more to her critical behavior. She apologized, said she missed him, and asked if they could date again. He held his ground and said no. She was devastated. I didn't make it easier on her by minimizing her behavior or blaming him. We talked about the consequences of actions. I told her that you don't always get second chances in romance, but you always get the chance to start over and get it right the next time. Over the course of the next year, something in her changed. She had to hit her bottom before she could finally address her fatal dating flaw, which she did by thinking before she spoke.

One night at a bar, Missy met a detective named Jay who really sparked her interest. Within weeks, some of the old, bad behaviors resurfaced. But she quickly learned to recognize and call herself on them before they could become problems. Being overly critical is the monster now contained in the box, the issue she knows she needs to watch. When she got married, she thanked me for getting her emotionally sober enough to say, "I do."

"All in a day's work," I told her, before sending her packing for the Tahiti honeymoon.

I've known and counseled several ladies with the title of Miss Overly Critical. I'm sure you recognize her modus operandi. She wants her guy to be tough when she wants him to be tough, tender when she wants him to be tender, and patient, of course, but not always. In fact, the key to her dating personality is that she looks for trouble. It's a variation of what my grandmother referred to as "negative attention seeking." She's scared to death but doesn't admit it. Instead of managing her fear, she lashes out. Miss Overly Critical wants her guy to put her in her place at the onset of her nitpicking. Otherwise, once her overly critical nature rears its ugly head, she'll run over him like a steamroller, squash his ego like a bug, and he won't know what hit him. If he doesn't shoot her down ASAP, then he's tagged as spineless.

The moral of this story is to think before you act or speak. Are you overly critical? Spend time figuring out what's motivating you to denigrate. Then remember that words are bullets and you can't take them back after you shoot a guy down.

Miss Overly Critical is not alone in the Miss Fatal Dating

Flaw competition. She is just one of several common contenders. Read on for the others in the Miss Fatal Dating Flaw competition:

MISS FAUX DESPERATION

"I wasn't really desperate, I guess I just acted that way." Those are words from Jamie, thirty-four-year-old writer, after she admitted her fatal dating flaw: acting needy post-date, especially in e-mails. Her confession came three days after what had seemed like a perfectly good night out on the town with a charming but emotionally unavailable entrepreneur. Well, it seemed good until she sent him a three-page e-mail leaving no emotional stone unturned two days afterward. Not surprisingly, the e-mail overwhelmed him with too much information delivered too soon, and they didn't continue dating. The irony of Jamie is that she's one of the least needy people I know. She travels the world, going on serious adventure trips to places like the Amazon for two weeks of swimming with anacondas. She loves her friends, family, and work. She has high (maybe overly so) standards for potential dates, especially when it comes to looks. But what happens to Jamie postdate seems to happen to a lot of women. Her behavior is the same with a stud or a dork; it doesn't matter. It can happen after a great date with a handsome charmer which ends with making out on a street corner under the moonlight. Or it can follow a rotten date where she listens to some schlemiel blather on about the fascinating life of an accountant. Soon after the date, Miss Faux

Desperation mysteriously overtakes Jamie's strong girl personality. She feels compulsion to act quickly, say too much too soon through long e-mails, and takes turns being alternately coy and then annoyed when the guy doesn't respond like she wants.

To help Miss Faux Desperation limit compulsive postdate follow up, I've created a strict dating diet, which includes the following three-step plan:

1. *The girl he meets is the girl he gets to date, at least for three months.* If he meets the strong girl, the one I refer to as the "real" one, that's the one he gets to hang out with for three months minimum. The other one, Miss Faux Desperation, must stay in her box until the right combination of drugs and self-esteem boost kick in. There are far too many cool, strong women like Jamie who don't realize how their behavior sometimes makes them seem needier than they really are.

2. *No e-mails.* No e-mail after a date is an absolute rule to be etched in stone. Drug addicts can no longer snort just a little cocaine now and then. Jamie is not allowed to send even simple e-mails after a date. It's too tempting to pontificate, ask too much, or reveal more than she should too soon. Period. She knows the consequences. If she breaks this rule, she knows I will come over and disconnect her computer.

3. *For every new first date, there must be a backup.* You have to have a backup date for every date you agree to go on, so that you don't put all your eggs in one basket.

This will eliminate some of the compulsive pressure you might feel. It doesn't matter if you troll the Internet and drag some loser from a chat room out to Starbucks for an hour. You must have a backup. Back in my prerelationship days, when I was dating a lot, there was no way I'd go out with some guy I was really interested in without having a backup. Guy Number Two was my safety net, frankly the only way I knew I'd relax and have a good time with Guy Number One. It's time for women to embrace the numbers aspect of dating like gay men do. Treat it less personally and more like gambling in Vegas. When the right one comes along, you'll know it. Two wrongs never make a Mr. Right. Don't end up so strung out from dating a string of Mr. Wrongs that you aren't ready when Mr. Right comes along.

MISS CONFUSED

Don't you love girls who talk tough about wanting sex without dating? I do. They say they want to date like a typical man. That is, they want to have sex at will and not get involved. I have known a few girls who can pull this off, but it's not usually the case. A more typical example is Cathy, who wore the crown of Miss Confused for almost a year. She's thirty-eight, tall, strikingly pretty, and really funny. Out of a marriage only six months, she was thrilled to jump on the dating bandwagon again.

So she hopped into an affair at work with Jean Paul, the

hottie who works on the same floor. He's from France and has maybe eight working brain cells.

It started out like a song, a sexy, languorous French ballad. Don't they all? "Dave, I am so excited to just have fun and not worry about getting involved," she told me one night over martinis. Coincidentally, so was he. This happy arrangement lasted all of a week until my phone rang at 11:00 p.m. In between the sobs, I managed to deduce that Mr. Hottie had said he was "maybe going to stop by that night," but he hadn't shown up. She felt so alone. She couldn't tell her girlfriends. Two of them would judge her and another one had the hots for Jean Paul herself, so her opinion would be biased. Obviously, she couldn't tell her ex-husband, mother, or coworkers. So she turned to me.

Cathy was Miss Confused. She said she wanted to have a fling like a boy, but she turned into a girl every time he didn't call back. I told her it's important to figure out not only what she wants, but also what works for her. Trying to turn Jean Paul into her sophisticated, continental boyfriend was a waste of time and tears. You can't turn mutton into lamb. I have done this so often with guys I was interested in, I should have a rainbow ribbon to commemorate my vain attempts. Contrary to popular belief, gay guys aren't always into constant flings and casual sex. I tell my gay friends who are searching for romance: don't try to turn tricks into boyfriends. It doesn't work.

The affair with Jean Paul Le Hottie at the office cooled. But when she's dating, Miss Confused still appears, and there's a conflict between what I call the "Cathy Light" and "Cathy Dark" sides of her personality. Cathy Light knows that she's only happy pursuing guys who are into more than just having sex with her. Cathy Dark thinks she can approach sex with what she considers typical male nonchalance. Cathy's behavior is no different than how I was when I was single and out there. As an admitted serial monogamist, casual dating took its toll on me, even when I felt it was important to be out there exploring. You want to be nonchalant but it's hard! Too bad there's not a magic pill you can take to switch on and off the two competing sides; one craving nonchalance and the other, real connection. A lot of talking and tears later, she's more self-aware and not so quick to take a nosedive into pain.

Before you dive into a casual, intimate relationship with a guy, be honest with yourself. Are you really willing to deal with the implications of a truly casual fling, such as random contact, no strings, and fleeting connection? Or are you acting the part of the swinging single? Figuring this out upfront will keep you from being Miss Confused.

MISS MISTAKE

Amy, a thirty-five-year-old banker, can cook a soufflé, balance a financial portfolio, and run four miles in twenty-eight minutes. She can do all of this in an afternoon. But when it comes to choosing men, she's absolutely hopeless. If Amy were presented with a lineup of ten men—nine of them in the normal range of human behavior and one a totally self-absorbed, grade A loser—do you want to guess which one she'd pick? Actually, "pick" isn't even the right word. Guess which one she'd hurl herself at with all the gusto of a pole-vaulter? That's an indication of just how strong her attraction to self-absorbed idiots was until she finally liberated herself from the evil clutches of her fatal dating flaw. I'd never seen a woman make such consistent mistakes with her man choices. Amy planned an introductory night out so that her friends could meet her latest loser, who got drunk and repeatedly called all of us by the wrong names before he slipped out the side door without saying good night to any of us. The problem wasn't that she'd forced a loser into our midst for an evening. The problem was that she defended him.

A similar situation happened when my forty-two-year-old friend Cathleen, blind to the vices of her boyfriend David, introduced him to her friends. David was obnoxious, self-absorbed, and made Cathleen miserable and anxious. Yet our typically confident and self-assured friend was at a loss with David. She lost her voice and herself. Our mutual friend Rose and I agreed that we had to think of a way to make sure Cathleen evaluated men differently from that point forward. Rose sternly said, "We're too old to be having these kinds of experiences." It worked. To this day, The David Debacle was her romantic waterloo. But no matter what happens with men now, I don't think she's ever going to lose her voice again.

I related to Amy and Cathleen's stories. They are common ones for gay men as well, tied to low self-esteem and the inability to define normal behavior. Being treated poorly or being ignored by a man seems like the most customary thing in the world when you don't think much of yourself. I decided some gay boyfriend tough love was in order. The gay Dr. Phil therapy I advocated for Amy focused on enforcing equal opportunity standards of behavior for all prospects. These norms included how every man should treat her, alone and around friends, and what types of behavior were appropriate for different levels of a relationship. For example, if he warrants more than casual date status, he has to step up to the plate. I asked her, "How would a girl who felt like a total winner react if the guy she was seeing didn't call her when he said he would?"

Her first reaction was a mousy, "She'd tell him she feels hurt." I moaned in disbelief, locked the door, and denied her food and water as if we were at a Werner Erhard EST session. I kept at her, repeating the question, "She'd do what?" until I had her yelling out with her fist in the air, "She'd blow the bastard off!"

Next, we earmarked character traits that she should she look for early on to red flag the terminally self-absorbed male. The good news is that she's happier now, and has no more loser dates—at least no second ones.

For Bobbi, it was a matter of seeing finally that she went for what she wanted, not necessarily what she needed. "I was always attracted to the exact antithesis of what I'd need. Even my husband, who was handsome, funny, and smart, was also a raging alcoholic and totally irresponsible. I loved that he was Mr. Party Guy. I dated bad, irresponsible boys who weren't in it for the long haul. Some women spend a lot of time thinking about what they're looking for, but I've never been a goal-oriented person. I just didn't focus my energy on that for myself."

How do you determine what's a potentially fatal dating flaw? And how do you curb it before it happens? You might have a fatal dating flaw if any of these ring a bell:

1. *Have More Than Two Guys Pointed Out the Same Flaw?* Usually, if you have a fatal dating flaw, someone knows it and has called you on it. Chances are that you just didn't want to hear it. Your clever mind has ways to dismiss the source and rationalize your behavior. But if more than two men have mentioned a certain unflattering characteristic to you, pay attention.

2. *Have You Sung the Girls' Version of "One for My Baby, and One More for the Road" Lately?* Have you ever ended a relationship due to the dating flaw and later regretted it? That's what happened to Missy. She'd regret her bad choices later and wonder why she acted the way she did with men she'd once liked. If you look back on a relationship, wish it hadn't ended, and know that one of your traits played a part in its demise, then it's time to work on that trait. You don't want to end up like Sinatra, hunched over a bar at 2 a.m., crooning "Set 'em up, Joe."

3. *Have You Tried Controlling the Fatal Dating Flaw, but Found Yourself Powerless as You Compulsively Commit It Yet Again?* Like an alcoholic with a drink, if you find that your best attempts at controlling the beast within, that nasty flaw that torpedoes your relationships, aren't working, consider a new option. Maybe it's time to check into the Betty Ford Center wing for emotional

dysfunction. Or perhaps more practically, become more aware of it, and censor your comments as you learn to modify your thoughts. Like Amy did, set up a system for benchmarking normal behavior so that you'll have a clearer way to evaluate men.

4. *Does Another Female in Your Family Have the Same Flaw?* Fatal flaws might not be genetic, but they are definitely hereditary. "I once bought a postcard that simply stated 'Everyone Is a Complete Disappointment,' and sent it to my sister, who'd said the same thing weeks earlier when her latest romantic tragedy occurred," said Liz. "That phrase was our flaw. By God if every man we met didn't live up to it!" After much soul searching, Liz now half-jokingly refers to herself as a "recovering malcontent."

5. *Do You Keep Thinking That Next Time, the Next Relationship Will Turn Out Differently?* The definition of insanity in Alcoholics Anonymous is "repeating the same dysfunctional behaviors over and over, and expecting a different result each time." There's nothing sadder than the woman who races into each new relationship only to find each one dissolve within weeks. While you can't take the blame for every relationship disappointment, learn from your mistakes so that you don't make the same ones twice.

2

YOU'RE NOT GOING TO MEET AN ELIGIBLE, STRAIGHT MAN AT COOKING CLASS

Where the boys are!

"I really have to meet more men," said Cathleen a couple of years ago. "So I've enrolled in a cooking class led by Mario Batali." I didn't get the logic. Mario Batali is an accomplished chef, to be sure. If you love cooking, then a cooking class by a master chef is, as Martha S. says, a good thing. On a side note, Cathleen's penchant for stalking celebrity chefs is a separate issue that needs to be covered in another book, preferably by someone with expertise in dealing with psychotic delusions. But, as I told her, "If your point is meeting eligible straight men, you have a greater chance of dating Julia Child than you do of meeting Mr. Right."

Follow your bliss. The mantra, credited to Joseph Campbell, pops up everywhere nowadays, from refrigerator magnets you find at your overpriced whole foods grocer, to scores of books on finding the right man, career, and spiritual path.

Following your bliss is a worthy goal. Just know it may not lead you to a worthy man.

So let's get one thing straight. Do you want to meet a cool straight guy? Then listen to me. Wise are the women who follow their bliss part of the time, and men the other. Follow the first rule of fishing: go where the fish are! Straight men hang out at pool halls. Is your bliss at a pool hall? Of course not. After months of no dates, should you skip seeing the girly flick with your gal pal in favor of having beers and hanging out with hustlers, sharks, and 8-balls? Of course.

I don't want you cruising to Alaska in search of ragtag construction workers making it their lives' work to create pipelines from Juneau to Baja. Yes, Alaska is one of those states where eligible men outnumber women by unreal odds like ten to one. Yes, the men of Alaska have been on Oprah, where desperate hopefuls hurl their business cards at men whose last female contact was probably pulling seals out of an oil spill. These guys even have their own Alaska Bachelors calendar. But I refuse to put you on the proverbial dating iceberg and set you out to sea. I want you to find love where you are, or at least the nearest metropolitan town within the contiguous forty-eight states. Sometimes you need to change your scene to change your mindset, so if you need a fun weekend as the belle of the ball in Alaska to gain confidence and pay attention to the best places to meet men, that's fine. But don't set up an igloo. Consider bringing the confidence and newfound knowledge back home with you.

When thirty-year-old Melissa was looking for a break

from her recently ended romance, she consulted a gay travel agent. "Here's the deal," she said boldly. "I am single, out of a bad relationship, and want to have fun and meet new guys." He immediately sent her packing with traveler's checks and suntan oil to Costa Rica, where the man to woman ratio was 3-1. Those are the kinds of odds a girl like Melissa needs. She doesn't need more "girl overload" events that were far too predominant on her schedule. In her words, "I was in a dead-end dating social situation. After I volunteered to cohost a singles event that was going to be five women to each man (the lucky bastards), my gay friend rolled his eyes and told me to find new places to meet guys. Single gals and racehorses wither under bad odds like that." So she went to Costa Rica, met tons of men, and had a fling with a hot local artist who also ran a kickboxing studio. Melissa got her groove back and learned the value of going where the boys are. When she returned home, meeting men was no longer a problem.

If there's one thing gay men know, it's how to find out where our kind hang out. Thanks to the Internet, careful planning, and a discerning, goal-oriented approach to spending our time, we find other gay men from New York to New Guinea. I want to help you do the same. Focus on where your kind hangs out. It's not always a matter of sacrificing your interests for the sake of meeting a man, either. Jenna managed to merge the two, with a little help.

"Charlie, my twenty-seven-year-old gay friend who's into indie rock, got me to volunteer for an alterative rock music festival in town," says Jenna, a twenty-six-year-old single girl in Seattle. "I met really cool guys who were creative but, amazingly, not gay. Every time I tried to be around creative guys, I was a magnet for the gay ones. Then again, I was really into theatre. Not that there aren't straight guys into theater, but Charlie made me see that the odds weren't in my favor. He led me away from theater toward the creative nongay guys who love music and writing. These festival boys were hip cool guys who got it. I ended up dating two of them at once and am really happy with one of them still after a few years."

"My gay friend James told me the secret to flirting at coffee shops and Internet cafes," says Lauren, a twenty-seven-year-old party planner in St. Louis. "We made it a game. I act like I have an agenda. It gives a certain attitude that is cool and busy, but hey, I am in a coffee shop so I am out there. As I work on my computer, I keep one eye open. If someone catches it and reciprocates, then bingo. It's an easy, casual setting to have a conversation. 'What are you working on?' is always a built-in icebreaker for the guy, too."

Sadly, the time-honored tradition of meeting men through matchmaking friends is fading fast in our busy, less-mannered era. In addition to bars, singles mixers, and friends, the following focus on places to meet eligible straight men, and what you can expect from each. Consider this advice from Jill, a twenty-nine-year-old restaurant manager from Atlanta, who told me, "Honey, I love your list. It's true that we need to find better places. I cannot bear another night out talking about men surrounded by five other women. I am not going to get lucky in a harem, sweetie!"

Sing it, sister.

But keep in mind that the winning combination is right

place plus right attitude. Stay cautiously open wherever you go. How can you avoid social situations that leave you with greater hope of finding Nemo than finding a worthy man?

1. *On a Clear Day You Can See Forever—So Clarify.* Why are you spending your time doing what you do? If your goal is to meet an eligible straight man, then rearrange your schedule (and maybe your priorities) to make sure you aren't filling all your time with straight-man-repellent activities.

2. *Follow the Rules of Vegas, and Go with Winning Odds.* Go to SMF (straight-man-friendly) destinations and boost your chances of meeting Mr. Right. You wouldn't put your money down on a horse with ten-to-one odds, would you? Why would you be as risky with your time, given the same odds for meeting an eligible guy?

3. *Avoid Pressure Cookers.* Bars, singles events, and blind dates increase pressure faster than a deep-sea diving adventure. Guess what else? Straight men, at least the kind you'd probably like, won't shine in those situations. Find activities and events where the social awkwardness will be diffused. Activities where you actually do something, whether it's participating in a class or going on a hike, are best. The truth is that straight men hate the awkward social situations possibly even more than you do.

4. *Be More Targeted than a Marketing Campaign.* Target isn't just a store. It's a crucial dating principle, vastly

underused by the populace. You want a thirty-three-year-old quiet Jewish doctor from Queens who likes contemporary art and squash? Make sure you state that to your friends and in personal ads, go the museums where you'd be likely to meet him, join a squash group at your gym. The man you seek isn't at a sports bar.

5. *Act "As If" You Are a Gay Man.* Enjoy yourself, don't project so much, and don't treat straight, eligible men as if they are white tigers at the zoo. As Washingtonian Carol says, "When I was single I pursued men like a gay man would pursue another gay man. By that I mean, without shame. My gay friend David validated that. David didn't encourage me to husband hunt. Part of it is a difference in ethos. Straight women often look for the father of the children and the husband. I decided to not approach men like that."

6. *It's Not All About You.* Of course it is in some ways, but not when it comes to a personal ad. When Jennifer, a thirty-two-year-old from North Carolina, wanted to create her ad on Match.com, she started it with "I want," followed by a laundry list of demands that no mere mortal could possibly fulfill. Her ad made her seem like an overzealous, overreaching, whiny, demanding Cinderella, but without the team of magic mice to get her to the castle on time. My advice to her was, "Make the ad about him. Then cut out half of your unreasonable demands. It wouldn't hurt to cut the whining and replace it with humor, either." We devised a better ad that began, "You are the type of guy

who . . ." followed by fun and reasonable criteria. She received twenty-five responses the first week.

Places to Meet Eligible Men: What You Can Expect

POOL HALLS. When you were younger, complaining about school or mean kids, maybe some nice adult appeased you with a trip to the ice cream store. Now as a single grown-up, complaining about your dating life, I will take you to an upscale pool hall. I have done this many times and it's often eye-opening for women who wouldn't ever dream of stepping into one for fear of soiling their pumps and reputation. Once inside, they see male-to-female ratios that inspire hope, not dread. It's a bar with games, and not the emotional ones. Not that all the boys are straight shooters (emotionally speaking, of course) but the odds are in your favor. Cue up!

GOLF COURSES. Fore! Any interest at all in eighteen holes or the driving range? Spend the afternoon in the sun with a bucket of balls. Golf courses and driving ranges are always overpopulated with men, and they go gaga over women who can show some style while they swing their sticks.

ADVENTURING CLUBS. Not only is there the getting-to-know-him-while-you're-both-distracted-by-activity advantage, but you'll also get a sense of his spirit and approach to fitness.

THE INTERNET. Dating on the Internet is like playing the lottery; so many chances, so few winners. But it's still the most immediate way for a girl to jump into the dating scene and get her feet wet. "Hope for the best and expect the worst," as thirty-year-old Match.com devotee Rachel says.

SPORTS VENUES. Unless it's the WNBA, with three lesbians for every straight man (bad odds unless you are considering switching teams), sports venues are an excellent place to experience men in their natural habitat. With their guards down, they're having fun and feeling good. What better time to survey the scene and evaluate who's worth your time? If sitting through an entire game seems dull or daunting, consider this. The It's Just Lunch higher-end dating service recently released this finding; 77 percent of men said they wouldn't mind leaving a game early if a date wanted to go. Finally, if you don't want to spring for tickets to the game, go to a sports bar on a key game night.

COED SPORTS. Sports like volleyball and kickball are great ways to participate in healthy joint activities to see if you're compatible. Best of all, you'll find out how he really feels about strong women. As thirty-five-year-old Sarah says, "Playing volleyball with a group of cool guys was the gateway to many dates. I saw how they related to women in a casual but competitively charged setting. I found out who was supportive and who was misogynistic. It was an excellent way to screen."

CONTINUING EDUCATION. As long as the class isn't Stitch and Bitch Needlepoint, the chances are good that you'll meet men in a classroom setting. Remember the fun grade school years of writing crush notes to boys, sideways glances from desk to desk, and the chance to explore guys on a regular basis over a period of months? He has to show up for this regular classroom date, or else he fails. All dates should have such consequences.

CHURCH. Don't let the fact that I met and dated the worst, most two-timing gay guy through church throw you off. This is a smart way to meet a man who will, at least, share your faith and values.

THE GYM. If nothing else, the gym is full of eye candy that you can enjoy without a sugar rush. At least you'll know you share a common interest in keeping up your bodies and managing stress. There's something very primal about meeting a guy in this setting. How can his defenses be up when he's in his gym shorts, sweating?

WORK. You could argue that work is not the sexiest venue for meeting guys. There's stress, pressure to perform, and deadlines. But not so fast. Meeting guys through work and career can be a smart dating move. If nothing else, you can explore his dating potential under the safe guise of developing your network of friends. No guy can knock your moxie for being a confident woman in a business setting. And by sharing your skills and interests, you might find common ground on more than just business issues. Keep in mind, too, that sometimes companies can act as a screener for dates, since they are good at selecting people and deciding who belongs to their tribe. In addition, work can be a launching pad for you to be "out there" in your profession at conferences, meeting vendors, and networking.

ROCK CONCERTS AND OTHER OUTDOOR EVENTS. If you think that "Good Charlotte" refers to a part the safe part of a downtown city in North Carolina, then maybe you need to immerse in the world of rock n' roll a little more. Any event where there's a band and vendors selling beer and those gigantic Fred Flintstone turkey legs (or some other meat-on-a-stick) is a straight boy stomping ground.

VIVA LAS VEGAS. You know that ad campaign tag line, "What happens in Vegas stays in Vegas?" It's true. I suggest Las Vegas as a testing ground for women who want to experiment with their more aggressive sides. Ladies, hit the blackjack tables. Play the vamp, flirt more outrageously than you normally might when you feel judgmental eyes upon you, and treat men like they're part of the overall entertainment package. They are. Remember, what happens in Vegas stays in Vegas. But the confidence you acquire travels home with you.

SPEED DATING. Speed dating is like a game of romantic musical chairs for grown-ups. Of course, you have to watch out for men with Social A.D.D. at these types of events. They thrive on three-minute bursts of interaction. Any man can shine for three minutes, so the real judge of speed dating is how they act later at a restaurant when no one should be in a rush. Respond to the instant chemistry rush of speed dating, but remember to keep your expectations in check. Adjust and apply courtroom rules when faced with speed daters: he's suspect until proven worthy.

THE BEACH. This is a tried and true alternative for women in need of a fast cure from a recent breakup or long, dry spell. Visit someplace crowded and sunny. (Mexico springs to mind.) The fabulous combination of sand and margaritas is the recipe for true love's giggly, immature cousin: infatuation. How many girlfriends and gay boyfriends can you squeeze into a hotel room and still have a ball? But beware the limitations of meeting on Fantasy Island if you are looking for something lasting. You don't go to Disneyworld expecting to take Goofy home with you.

COFFEE SHOPS AND INTERNET CAFES. Get wired with caffeine as you cruise oh-so-surreptitiously. Welcome to the world of the casual cruise scene so familiar to gay guys. Make sure you have a socially acceptable distraction (i.e. reading a book or typing on your computer) that allows you to keep one eye on the screen and one eye on the scene. Why should you feel self-conscious? You're *working*, after all. Right? Of course you are, honey.

BLACK-TIE EVENTS. Yes, Cinderella, when the shoe fits, black-tie events can be fun and exciting new ways to meet men. I have met a few princes who bat for my team at black-tie events, and it's a glamorous start. But, as forty-two-year-old black-tie affair veteran Cathleen notes, "The downside is that you might meet a guy whose first love is the social thrall. I did, and it got old really fast." After twenty black-tie events full of "hypersocializing" but devoid of intimacy, you'll be longing for midnight when you magically return to the quiet fireplace.

VOLUNTEERING. What better way to meet a great guy than through volunteering? Right away, you know that he's into something more than just himself and that you share at least one common interest.

ANYWHERE WHEN YOU AREN'T LOOKING. After noting above all the places to meet men, it's important to remember that the best rapport sometimes comes with the least planning. So many women I know have met their Mr. Right in line at the supermarket, at a restaurant bar waiting for another date, or running in the park, sans makeup or single girl persona. Like many gay men, I am a big believer in irony. Love does appear when you aren't looking too hard.

3

ARE YOU WASTING YOUR TIME AND PERFUME?

Ways to tell if your hot prospect plays for
your team.

Thanks to smarter girls, more out and proud boys, and gay boyfriends who police the straight dating ranks for their girlfriends and out the closeted brethren who try to date women, we see fewer tragic cases of "Oh my God, I dated a gay man! I should have known." As Paula, a twenty-nine-year-old agent asks, "To my knowledge, I never dated a gay man, unless you count the prom. Does that count?" No, it doesn't. But high school prom is the last acceptable time that you are allowed to date a gay man, unless there are mitigating factors (i.e. family fortune) or you are purposefully taking a much-needed Diet Coke break after too much of the "real thing" (after all, a girl can't be expected to date serially without some time off). Of course, there are still occasional slip-ups and you shouldn't feel bad if you have ended up thinking Brad was Mr. Right only to discover that Brad plays for the other team.

Liza Minnelli, Carrie Fisher, and 50 percent of the women married to soap opera actors know exactly what I am talking about, don't you, ladies? A few of my girlfriends have come to this sad realization, too.

"After a fun few dates full of laughter and sexy flirting, things progressed to my place. He cried in bed. A red flag, obviously. I know I am not *that* good, so something had to be up with him," said Rachel, a twenty-seven-year-old New Yorker. "Looking back, I could tell by the first few kisses that something was missing in the passion. But he was very cute so I decided to go further. Big mistake. I should have called you first." Yes, I told her, you should have. Then again, "Shoulda, coulda, woulda."

Backed by sound advice from her gay best friend, sometimes a girl has to put two and two together to avoid a three-dollar bill. "I was dating this guy who turned out to be gay. He never told me. I had to tell him," said Lisa, a twenty-nine-year-old creative director in Virginia. "It wasn't exactly an outing. In fact, I think he wanted to get caught. He must have! He took a Kiehls beauty product basket to a bachelor party for his male friend, for God's sake. Afterward, I told him, 'Uh, take an aged bottle of Scotch the next time, and oh, by the way, you are so totally gay.' It was briefly awkward. But that was the end of dating and the start of a great friendship." If a woman finds out before getting entrenched in dating expectation, then maybe it's not so hard to be friends. Often, it doesn't work that way, and they find out too late.

I can relate to women in this position. I actually dated a guy who told me he was really straight after way too long a period to hold on to a key nugget of information like that. Of course, what he meant to say was "confused," but the word came out "straight" (no pun intended). As Sharon Stone once said, "Women may fake orgasms, but men can fake whole relationships." When you're dating, you expect to hear that someone wants his or her space, or is seeing someone else or doesn't want the same level of dating you want. But after romantic weekends and making plans for the future, you just don't expect them to say that you aren't even the right sex. So I empathize.

It's even harder for women these days since women are embracing their power more and more, while straight men are experiencing a sort of style renaissance. It's an interesting combustion of forces at work. The rules, if you will, are out the window, despite what the author of that old-fashioned rules book tells women. Fewer men and women want to be as limited to stereotyped, outdated notions of what they should be.

Three women I respect and admire all recently said, in effect, "I want a man who's just gay enough." What they meant is that they want a man who's sensitive and stylish enough to capture their minds, but straight as Cupid's arrow when it comes to capturing their hearts and touching their bodies. Be careful for what you wish for. Because the "is he or isn't he?" gay man we saw too much of in the 80s is back in full force, updated with twenty-first century spiffy clothes, soft feelings, and questionable attitudes. He's currently known as a metrosexual. There's no question that he's "gay enough," but is he "straight enough," too?

THE METROSEXUAL. A metrosexual is defined in the new world lexicon as a typically urban man who is heterosexual but proudly enjoys stereotypically gay male things like shopping, pampering, sensitivity, and paying attention to the details of romance. He knows the day when the new line of Ugg boots will be available in this country. He knows the carbohydrate count of every item on the menu when you dine out. He is likely to apply a variety of hair gels and mousses, and even use the term "product," a word once the sole domain of beauty stylists, to describe his hair and grooming aids. I remember being shocked the first time I saw a heterosexual male do this on television. It was *The Bachelor* reality dating show (a metrosexual haven if ever there was one) and Bob Guiney, the bachelor referred to himself as a "product whore."

"And some women just love him," I sighed to no one in particular. I knew that in some strange way, the world had shifted. It would be more freeing in some ways, but also possibly more confusing for straight women. It used to be that if your skin regimen didn't take at least three times as long as your boyfriend's, then you just knew he was gay. Even the postfeminist–era sensitive male, referred to as the "Alan Alda," didn't call himself a product whore. Nor did he consider pedicures with paraffin wax treatment his straight male birthright.

Now with metrosexuality, I believe that straight single women are, once again, "holding out for a hero," as Bonnie Tyler implored them to do on the soundtrack to the film *Footloose*. They want a straight guy who is hard on the outside but soft on the inside.

The twenty-first century "is he or isn't he?" man is more socially integrated than the 80s version. One of the great virtues of a more closeted, condemning society, for straight women at least, was that secretly gay men had the decency to act more ashamed. Ah, the bravado that they show now! How dare they? And how can a girl tell who's what anymore? Clubs are more mixed. Young boys raised by post-60s feminist moms grew into young men a tad more aware and willing to express their feelings. There really are a few honestly straight, never married men over forty. Even the gays don't feel compelled to like Barbra Streisand anymore. And, socially, men are more objectified now, which means that more of the straight ones dress better and work out. What is this? Europe with its blurred lines of gender?

The answer is two words: David Beckham. He has been dubbed "Mr. Skirt" by the British press. With carefully plucked eyebrows, a body straining at the seems of overly tight and revealing clothes, and tinted sparkling hair highlights, he spends weekends in the country with Elton John and partner, "gancing" the night away ("gancing" is the phenomenon of straight men who like dancing with other men). The absolutely gorgeous Mr. Skirt is also a studly soccer player with a hot wife, and, at times, a confusing, gender-bending flirt. We have to get used to the idea that Europeans flirt with women and men. So maybe there's a Euro Clause, sort of like a Eurorail pass for sexual ambiguity, where he gets a free ride to girl- or boyland if he's from Italy, Spain, England, or France. As my friend Brian says, "Throw all the rules out the window with Europeans."

THE NARCISSIST. Even if he's metrosexual (whew, what a relief), then you still have to worry that he might also be a narcissist, which is actually worse. Yes, it's true. Those wonderful, modern-man traits, like beating you to the spa to get a seaweed wrap so his skin will glow more than yours, canceling the date with you because he needs to stay in and massage his aura, and the nagging feeling you get when you're on the phone with him that conversations are all one-sided, and that he considers your part of the conversation merely a time for him to regroup before speaking again, are red flag warnings that you may be in the presence of a modern male narcissist. If such red flags apply to your man, I hereby give you a marching order to arch that eyebrow and keep it there until you have 100 percent verification that he's straight or at least above an eight on the Kinsey sexuality continuum scale. Then you have to decide whether catering to a man who'll probably spend the rest of your lives glancing past you to the mirror is worth it.

When one of my best friends, Cathy, started dating thirty-two-year-old, dark-haired Greg with the beautiful smile, she was so excited. "Dave, he's so handsome, funny, stylish, a little sexually reserved, and he does Yoga, too," she exclaimed.

How many red flags did *you* count in her sentence? I was up to three when I answered her. "Great, can't wait to meet him." I took the two of them to a gay friend's birthday party and watched Greg like a hawk while Cathy talked to the other guests. I checked off what I thought were questionable traits. His shoes were polished like a salesman's, every strand of his hair was perfectly in place, and he insisted on being front and center in every picture taken, flashing the same studied smile (in fact, we nicknamed him "Mr. Pictures").

Worse, he delighted in telling me about the pedicure and sea-weed body scrub he'd gotten earlier that day because, in his damning words, "I want to be presentable to the women in hot-yoga class."

During the night, Cathy whispered to me a few times, "I really like him, but I can't figure him out. He doesn't seem that interested in me sexually, but he wants to hang out with me all the time."

I almost responded, "He's gayer than a night at *Disney Skaters on Ice*," but I stopped myself. I also wanted to stop Cathy from pulling a Liza Minnelli. How would I be able to live with myself if I did nothing (too bad Liza's real friends didn't feel the same when she said 'I do' to her latest gay hubby)? But then I caught him checking out another girl's boobs, only to interrupt his drooling stare by catching his own reflection in the mirror. Hello, Narcissus! For the rest of the night, I kept track of the five times he checked himself in the mirror. A certain Carly Simon tune ran through my mind as I whispered to Cathy, "Congratulations, you are dating a narcissist. He's so vain, he probably thinks the song is about him." The man even proudly confessed that his top priority for high school prom night was to make sure he tanned his penis. That's right. As you and I were nervous getting our first formal wear, Greg was confidently strutting into Casa Del Sol with his SPF 15 lotion, ready to apply it "down there." Apparently, narcissism starts young!

It all added up. He wasn't gay. He was straight. But he was a narcissist. The narcissist card always trumps both the straight and gay cards. Of course he loved being around Cathy. She adored him. He lived off that. She confused it with interest. It took her about two more weeks but she finally saw the light and let him go. Of course, that's easier said than done with a narcissist. They are very hard to break up with, much harder than regular men. It's not that they care about the relationship with you, or will even miss you personally. It's just that devoted followers are so hard to find in these busy times. They can't stand not to be the center of attention. Even worse, as I found when calling him "narcissist" to his face, they are extremely hard to insult. It gets harder and harder to put them down. Every insult is more attention. To this day, Greg still calls Cathy, hoping perhaps to see more of himself in the limpid, reflecting pools of her eyes.

PARASITE SHARKS AND FAUX FAGGING SHARKS. Just when a girl thought it was safe to go back in the water, so to speak, there are two new species of male sharks in the ocean. The first is the parasite shark. This breed feeds off of his gay host to get to the hot women attached to the gay host. More confusing than metrosexuality is the relatively new concept of "parasite dating," where straight men use gay men as a stepping stone. Some straight men have figured out that they are extra hot and desired if we gay guys think they're hot. So they use us as a stepping stone. We are their pass, their entrée to the exclusive cool girl club. With us, they are "on the list." Wearing their fake I-love-my-cool-gay-friend persona, their eyes survey the waters looking for the right prey, the hot girl who gives a straight man extra credit when he relinquishes homophobia and enjoys the company of gay men.

The second is the straight shark who plays gay to win

your affection, when in reality he is a snake in expensive lambswool clothing, probably with a designer label from the Barneys biannual warehouse sale. We call this the faux fagging shark. These boys are smart. They have their own version of gaydar, which helps them go where the hot girls are. They realize the power of getting two steps ahead with Ms. Sexy, who lets down her guard with gay guys because she can trust them. Call this a form of sexual nepotism; it's moving up the ladder quickly through association with a "brother."

To the straight boy sharks who might be reading this for secret tips on how to get the hot girl (the same straight boys who want to hang around when I am out with my hot girlfriends), I say this: Faux fagging and parasite dating are not cool. It's cool if you want to be metro. Indulge your inner spa boy. See and be seen in the coolest places. Relate better to women and reap the benefits. But if you pull the wool over her eyes to take advantage and make her think you are more sensitive and caring than you really are, I'll make sure you get double vision before you try it again.

YOU NEED GAYDAR! The point is that I cannot stand by and let my girls get blindsided. I am all for exploration and men finding themselves, but not at the expense of you! I know where my loyalty lies and it's not with bi boys as they slide down the transitional slippery slope to gayland. It's time to point out ways for you to determine if your potential Mr. Right bats for your team. Gay men have to know who's on our side. After all, there are fewer of us in the general population, so if we want to find each other we must pay close attention. After years of assigning men to one team or another based on looks, personal traits, or that unexplainable "sixth sense," my gaydar is honed and at your disposal.

I've played the game Who Will Get the Next Guy when a girlfriend and I are walking down the street. We try to be subtle. We are certainly subtler than the construction workers who make catcalls at every chick who saunters by. But Who Will Get the Next Guy is an eye-opening game for some women. They get to see men through the eyes of their gay friends. Twenty-seven-year-old Missy is a perfect example. "When I walk down the street with Evan (her hot twenty-eight-year-old gay friend in Chicago), I notice more about guys. Do they check me out, or Evan? You learn more when someone is confronted with a clear choice."

"My friend Johnny is an expert at picking out the gay men," said Barb, twenty-nine-year-old self-confessed gaydar-free woman in sunny Florida. "I don't know why I didn't get gaydar," she told me. "I am clueless to signs that a guy is closeted or ambiguous. But Johnny was closeted for so long; he came out at twenty-eight. That's why I think his gaydar is so honed. When he was in denial and shame about being gay, he'd have to rely on glances, body language, and vibes to connect with other guys like him, which I am sure he was desperate to do. He developed a sixth sense. It's second nature to him, and he's rarely wrong. Now when we are out and an attractive man is in range, I rely on Johnny to give him the gaydar check."

I want to leave my cool girlfriends with some clear-cut guidelines on how to wade through the seas of metrosexuals and narcissists, as well as faux fagger and parasite sharks, and reach the safer shores of dating. So before you visit www.straightacting.com or go on a reality TV show like Bravo's *Playing It Straight*, where one poor woman has to figure out which male contestants on a dating show are straight or gay, here are the tips to make sure your Mr. Right is right for you and not the gay softball league.

1. *The Nonpassion of the Sexless Boyfriend*. Ever had a man tell you, "Not until we're married, honey?" Did it seem like that frustrated him? There are probably only five men in the U.S. who are truly sexually saving themselves for marriage. This includes both Monica Lewinsky sex as well as going all the way. If you've been dating a while and, after all your pleadings, you aren't making it to third base, maybe a light bulb should go off. While I admire the abstinence-loving men, I can't imagine you wouldn't sense a real conflict from them when they say "no." So, if he seems all too happy to use the, "Not tonight, honey, I have a headache" excuse, throw out your red flag.

2. *When the Gentleman Is Too Gentle*. Never thought you'd be learning a lesson from *Gone with the Wind* in this book, did you? Well, here it is. Gentlemen who are too gentle will frustrate a girl to death. Ashley Wilkes certainly frustrated poor old Scarlett O'Hara right out of her corset and into the arms of Rhett Butler, where she would have stayed happy if she had read this book first. The truth is, a gentleman who is too gentle could be covering up the fact that, religious or social reasons

aside, he'd rather be buying "Gentleman and Gentleman" towels instead of focusing on you.

3. *He's Too Uptight Around Gay Guys*. It's cliché, but true. Real men who are comfortable in their own masculinity don't spend time knocking gay guys. First, that's a really stupid way to alienate all the hot girls who are loyal to their gay friends. Second, to paraphrase Macbeth, "The guy doth protest too much." Even Howard Stern, though no beacon of light for the enlightened, at least gets this right. His response to the eighteen-to-thirty-year-old *Beavis'n'Butthead*–loving straight boys who call in to his radio show and knock gay guys is, "Dude, what's your problem? Anyone who spends so much time busting on gay guys is gay. Dude, you are gay." Or, as my niece Amy says, "If he's homophobic, he either secretly gay or he's a closed-minded insecure loser who's not worth my time."

4. *The "Dancing Queen" Test*. Take him out dancing, let loose, and if he ever moves around with his hands in the air, chances are your man is a dancing queen. Straight men, even metrosexuals, dance with their hands down. Or if you are ballroom dancing and you start to feel that he is competitive with you about dipping, maybe you should follow his lead and let him go.

5. *Ask and Ye Shall Hear*. Due to pervasive heterosexism, it may not occur to some women that their man could be a walking, talking three-dollar bill. To counter this, I ask you to reconsider the simple maxim we all learned

as children. Assume and you make an ass of you and me. If you are reading this, you probably trust the opinion of your gay best friend. That means you are willing to hear the truth. So why not seek it out? Don't tell me after you find out your date is gay that you had questions you never asked. Ask now, and hopefully you'll avoid surprises later.

6. *Swim Safely to Avoid the New Breed of Sharks.* Next time you are sailing along having a perfectly good time meeting new straight guys with your gay friend present, ask him to check the waters to make sure they are free of faux fagger and parasite sharks.

4

SECRET, DEAD-END AFFAIRS: YOU'RE ONLY ALLOWED ONE

I hate hanging notes on your bathroom
mirror reminding you that he's never, ever
going to call back!

He's so hot. I know. His butt fills out a pair of jeans like
nothing you've ever seen short of a Calvin Klein ad. Your
mother would tell you to avoid him and behave yourself.
Your girlfriends would empathize with your roving eyes and
weak knees but, for reasons only known to them, make more
of your flirtation than it deserves. It's a curious form of girl-
on-girl sabotage that I've witnessed. If they're jealous of the
sexual heat between you and Mr. Dead-End Affair Hottie,
what better way to throw a wrench into your plans than by
playing the Puritan card? They'll remind you how you
whine about not finding a real relationship. They'll ask you
where the relationship is going. They'll blather on that dead-
end affairs are always bad detours.

I know better. I know my girl inside and out. Gay men are
still men after all and, whether it's fair or not, we are social-

ized to accept and act on our sexual needs. Now it's time for me to pass the baton and help you accept yours. You need a fling. It's been way too long, he's way too hot, and Mr. Long Lasting Relationship apparently took a wrong turn at Albuquerque because he's about three years overdue, according to your schedule.

I'm going to give you the special emotional dispensation you need, because who better than a gay man to help you compartmentalize dueling needs for Mr. Right and Mr. Right Now. Now, don't ask me repeatedly for this special dispensation. I'll be as withholding as the Pope if I feel you are misusing it. But when you are truly in need of external permission, I'll be there.

But I also know the pitfalls you'll face. Midway through this dead-end affair, your inner good girl will surface and, next thing you know, you'll be applying the old rules of dating. You'll forget why you got into this affair in the first place. You'll become obsessed with fitting the square peg that is him into the round hole that represents the relationship you mistakenly think you can force.

New Yorker Paula knows all about the quandary of bad boys when it comes to finding a boyfriend. "What is so appealing about inappropriate men?" she asks rhetorically. The simple answer is that they are the embodiment of a sometimes-necessary rebellion as well as an antidote to overly good girl syndrome.

"It's hard to admit now, but I actually saw boyfriend material in a drunken, older roadie whose two goals in life were late night partying and setting up lighting for R.E.M."

I know. I have been there. I have had several affairs with

the kinds of hot men that Kelly Clarkson sings about in her song "Beautiful Disaster." You know the type. They are hot, hypnotic magic men who come and go quicker than the wind.

Mortified that she once needed advice to get over losers, Paula says, "My gay best friend, Steven, gave me the best advice for moving on from the beautiful disasters. First, stop going to the 'bad place,' as he called it. It was the local bar, my dysfunctional version of the *Cheers* hangout, where basically the same guys with no potential showed up night after night. Second, don't give up. Keep thinking of new ways to find the right guy."

If you are stuck in a pattern of hooking up with the wrong guys, don't give up. Get active. There's a wonderful Buddhist phrase that translates roughly into: "Salvation begins when you realize there could be another way." In other words, you're on the right track when you consider more positive ways to connect with men who meet your needs. They won't all be Mr. Rights. But you can raise the bar (or leave the bar, in Paula's case) so that you won't waste your time. And when there are slip-ups, don't get too down. Consider them learning experiences. I won't say, "I told you so." I know that's judgmental and you get enough of that from other people in your life. So instead, let me give you the advice you need for getting yourself back on track, out of Never-Never Land, and certainly out of the victim mindset that's often easy for women to lapse into, thanks to years and years of societal "good girls don't" training.

As Rachel, a twenty-seven-year-old editor in New York, says, "My gay friend Mark is so upfront about having a good time to just have a good time. He dates without shame. I have learned from that. I can do what he does but in my own way. Do what pleases you. Quiet that little voice women sometimes hear that says 'Why would he buy the cow if he can get the milk for free?' Women have an agenda for dating, and we treat this agenda as if we are headed for an IPO. Mark and the gay guys I know don't worry so much. But I think it comes from the old wives' tale that sex is a power struggle. The girl wins if she gets the ring and the relationship. The boy wins by getting laid. We have to change this perception."

Despite the newfound freedoms we experience, we still have a few more mountains to climb when it comes to moving on from limitations imposed on us by societal expectations. Gay men still have to put on hiking books and get over the hills. So do straight women. We have to forge our own paths and not rely on the outdated trail markings to get us there.

Feeling a little like Hamlet, wondering aloud, "To fling or not to fling?" Here are strategies for making smart choices when that question makes you as confused as Shakespeare's Danish prince.

1. *Choose Your Fling Carefully: Avoid Long-Term Potential.* Of course, unless it's some momentary loss of taste (God, I hope not.), you will choose your flings carefully. But here's why it's especially important. You want to minimize pain when your paths cease to cross. Flings are sometimes best with someone you feel possesses no long-term potential. We all attribute certain characteristics to our ideal long-term partner. Try to

avoid these in a fling so you won't feel you're missing out when it's time to say good-bye.

2. *Be on the Lookout for Wayward Seagulls.* The type of man who loves and leaves is what I not so affectionately refer to as a "seagull dater." That is, a man who flies over you, looks better from a distance, swoops in, makes a lot of noise, craps on everything, and then leaves. Unfortunately, seagull daters are not just limited to seaside communities, as their name would lead you to believe. They can be found in all sorts of dry locales: mountains, prairies, and even landlocked urban environments where there's not so much as a stream. So if you are not sure whether you can handle the "love 'em and leave 'em" seagull dater, then proceed slowly and cautiously with all new prospects, until they show signs of roots and wings.

3. *Enjoy It While It Lasts.* There's nothing worse than splurging on a really rich, carb-laden meal with someone who's whiny and guilt-ridden. That makes you want to take your super-sized bowl of pasta, with the usually off-limits white flour, sugar, and trans fats, and dump it in her lap. The same applies to the dead-end affair. Enjoy every fattening minute, and tell yourself the same things you say when confronted with the cheesecake you've been saving up for after a long diet: A) Damn, this is tasty, B) I won't make it a habit, and C) I'll reinstate my willpower tomorrow.

4. *Change the Television Channel in Your Head.* Take the remote control, point it at your brain, and switch from

Lifetime (television for abused women and the gay men who love them) to the Reality Network. He didn't betray you. Betraying you would imply that he promised you something. He didn't. He signed on for an affair and he thought you did, too. The stalker-in-training whose inner Bridezilla now flares is a new person to him. She's much different than the cool, hot girl he met. You made a choice with eyes wide open. Put Bridezilla back in her box.

5. *(If It Ends Badly) A Girl Kisses a Few Toads on the Way to Her Prince.* Approach every relationship that ends as a learning experience. Romances with men are the curriculum you'll need to determine what's right for you and what isn't. I'd prefer if you'd learn quickly and easily, rather than at the school of hard knocks. Of course, you don't want to have too many diplomas on your wall. But if you learn from each and every relationship, then you are bound to refine your tastes, hone your character judgment and learn the warning signals for romantic time-wasters.

6. *(If It Ends Well) Every Girl Needs a Few Memories That Are Hers Alone.* This isn't a topic most of us discuss much, especially once we settle down. But the truth is that our memories of hot, past romances can keep us warm on a cold winter's night. None of us know what the future holds, so our job is to make the most of the present. As we get older, our memories make us feel like we have lived fully.

7. *Someday, We'll Look Back on This, Laugh Nervously, and Change the Subject.* During a summer visit with grad school friend Karen and her family, her husband, Mitch, asked me what she was like back then. It was a simple enough question, but I will never forget the look Karen shot me, her eyes were narrowed daggers full of foreboding. I suppose her mind raced with images of the two of us gallivanting around New York City, wreaking havoc on the straight and gay male population. The havoc was equal opportunity, I might add. Now this married mother of two worried that I'd spill the beans on men, martinis, outrageous flirtations, late nights, and last calls. I hesitated for all of ten excruciating seconds before answering, "We had fun, but compared to most twenty-somethings in New York, it was tame." I didn't lie. In the New York nightlife that I recall, running naked down Seventh Avenue followed by angry "trannie hookers" would've been considered tame, too. So, don't worry. When our life circumstances change and the past comes up, I will keep your secrets as if we were a collegial secret society. In fact, we were.

As you set out on an emotional and sexual journey to find yourself, just be careful. Very few people are able to handle the no-strings-type encounters without some fallout.

The GBN (Gay Boyfriend Network) is introducing a new system to help alert your support system when your emotional security is threatened by a dating situation. The new system, called *SASSE* (*Security Alert System for Spiraling Emotions*, pronounced "Sassy"), is your guide for what to do when he doesn't call soon enough, gives you a mixed signal, or vanishes completely after what you thought (and he said) was an awesome date.

The following threat levels each represent an increasing risk of emotional spiraling based on the threat of PDW (Post-Date Weirdness) or BBB (Bad Boyfriend Behavior). Next to each level are Suggested Protective Measures, designed by your gay boyfriend to help you survive and even thrive during each threat level.

SASSE
(security alert system for spiraling emotions)

SEVERE (HOT RED). A Severe alert means that the worst of dating trouble is imminent or has just happened. Your hunch was right. You should have trusted your instincts all along. Either he's just not into you or he's found someone else. You are not expected to maintain a Severe level for more than a week. It is a proven fact that human beings cannot sustain adrenaline.

All key personnel are redirected to your place to mobilize you. That means your gay boyfriend is with you during this period. You shouldn't be alone. Also make sure you fill your free time with close friends because after a crisis, you really need to distract yourself.

Emergency response mechanisms include:

- Lockdown on your home and personal space. Only top-level security clearances, such as your gay boyfriend and absolutely closest, trust-them-with-state-secrets girlfriends are allowed to enter the restricted area.

- Immersion in bad movies and cheap reality television. You need to see people who are in worse circumstances than you.

- Complete and total abandonment of food and alcohol restrictions unless you are in a 12-step program, in which case, your gay boyfriend should know to take you to meetings. Twice daily if necessary during the first critical week.

HIGH (BRIGHT ORANGE). A High alert is declared when you have enough bad male dating behavior to go on; the facts are indisputable. The calls aren't being returned, or if they are, there's coolness on the other end. It's harder to make plans with him and you feel the pressure is always on you. There's a high risk that you are headed for an emotional attack.

At this stage, your gay boyfriend should know not only the complete summaries of your dating interactions, but also should be kept aware of every interaction or, in the case of a "vanisher," how long it's been since your prospect has avoided contact with you.

Emergency response mechanisms include:

- Coordinating your key support system, including your gay boyfriend and closest other friends (we'll refer to them as "civilians" to make the distinction) just in case there really is a problem.

- Taking additional precautions in public in case you run into the guy. Your gay boyfriend should coach you on nonchalant ways to handle any public interaction so that you will maintain optimum dignity.

- Restriction of social activities to only those who really support you. The so-called friends, acquaintances, and competitive associates who can't be trusted to keep you feeling good (you know who they are!) must be kept at bay during this vulnerable time.

ELEVATED (SUNNY YELLOW). An Elevated alert is declared at the moment when you get that queasy feeling that something might be amiss in the dating department but you don't really have any evidence to go on, and the slight strain of paranoia could just be signs of PMS.

Your gay boyfriend should be alerted, however, in order to be prepared in case the level moves up to Orange. At this stage, you need not make any changes to your schedule or interactions with others.

Emergency response mechanisms include:

- Keeping track from this point on of unusual dating behavior and noting it for future reference.

- Immersion in your workout to clear your head and change the subject. While puffing away at the gym, listen to your "inner gay boyfriend" tell you that it's probably nothing, you are getting concerned over nothing, and that there's a payoff with straight men sometimes when you just play it a little emotionally cool.

- Have lunch with your gay boyfriend and remind yourself how other Elevated alerts have amounted to nothing.

GUARDED (SKY BLUE). The irony of this level blue is that you probably aren't feeling blue at all. It's just another day in dating land. Maybe you aren't over the moon at the moment, but things are proceeding normally for whatever dating stage you happen to be with this particular prospect. Of course, there's always that little voice in the back of your head that says, "Don't get too relaxed. After all, it's dating and by the very definition of the word, it's uncertain."

But there's no reason to do anything but go about your business normally, dismissing any thoughts of dating gloom and doom. It's easier said than done if you've had recent bad experiences. But your gay boyfriend will be able to reassure you at this stage that you are on track and everything's fine.

Response mechanisms include:

- A very generic, brief review of "dating gone wrong" contingency plans with your gay boyfriend.

- Awareness and appreciation of the calm. Remind yourself how great it is to not be at a higher level of alert.

- A thorough self-review of your own dating behaviors and actions thus far in the process. Happy with how you are behaving? Anything you think you want to tweak? Now is the time to consider those things.

LOW (TRANQUIL GREEN). This level means smooth sailing, a very low risk of emotional attack. Whether you've just met and you both see starts in each other's eyes, or you've been dating for months and it's all progressing so simply and easily, congratulations! This is an excellent time for your gay boyfriend to go on vacation, even taking an extended trip to somewhere far away, such as Australia, where emergency contact devices such as cell phones and faxes aren't easily accessible.

Ensuring that your gay boyfriend and other key personnel in your closest social support system receive proper training on the SASSE system is essential. Don't wait until you hit ELEVATED, and need to mobilize quickly. Plan ahead so that, during the time when you need them most, your closest advisors will be there to guide you through the hell of dates gone wrong, men who vanish after what you thought was a great time, and other emotionally destructive times.

Follow the SASSE system to ensure you have the protection you need for each level, and that all reasonable measures are taken to mitigate your vulnerabilities to emotional attack.

5

LIVE REPORT FROM THE LOCKER ROOM

Gay men who share gyms with straight
men answer those questions you've been
dying to ask.

Several girlfriends have asked me to tell them what men talk
about behind closed doors.

- "Is locker room talk all about boobs, movies, cars, and
  sports?" (Yes, pretty much.)

- "What do they say about us when we aren't around?"
  (Read on.)

- "I'd like to know how important the whole blow job thing
  is to guys. Because it's really not that much fun for us, so
  if it's not essential and regular sex is preferable, maybe I
  can just go with that?" (Um, it is important. Very. Sorry.)

- "Do men have a problem with women professionally?
  Are there men who really make bad comments about fe-

male coworkers, don't think women are as capable as men, and/or don't want to work with women or for women? Is the boys' club still strong?" (Some do. Yes. And, unfortunately, yes.)

These are typical questions I have gotten from women who want a peek inside the private mind of the average straight American male.

Do you think gay men are in the men's locker room compulsively checking out other guys? We aren't, and we resent the implication that we are sex-crazed animals. Checking out guys is occasional and usually subtle. What you might not realize is gay guys have little patience for the "bug-eyed locker room aficionados" who've given us a bad name all these years. Most of us just do our thing and keep to ourselves. But one thing is certain. We can't help eavesdropping on straight guys' conversations so that we can provide periodic intelligence updates from the frontlines of hetero male behavior. It's not even eavesdropping. How can it be when straight men bellow from across the locker room floor to each other as they do? If they're going to talk that loudly, then I have no problem listening and then bringing you the news straight from the very bastion of straight male openness, the locker room.

You could buy the information from me. But I can't put a price tag on some of the gems I've overheard. In my more than twenty years of sharing locker rooms with straight men, I could write a book just on their utterances. Luckily, I'll offer you the skinny for free. Over the years, I have heard comments in locker rooms that have made my skin crawl, temperature boil, titillation factor grow exponentially, and sense of propriety melt. Imagine the very best and most open dialogue from *Sex and the City* translated into straight male lingo and you'll have an idea what I'm talking about.

Of course, I have also been bored to tears. As you already suspect and I will confirm, male locker rooms are full of bravado. It's the equivalent of bragging girl talk. Imagine your boyfriend overhearing lunch with your shallow girl-friends. You'd be embarrassed, but probably less by shared intimate details than by monotony.

Nevertheless, to borrow the most overused phrase from the dot com era, I'm going to "lift the kimono" now and re-veal the more pertinent revelations, along with what you should learn from them. Here are the top ten things you need to know, live from the locker room:

1. *When He Talks About His Dates, They Don't Mean Much*. Yes, guys are full of bravado. There's talk of games won, worlds conquered, envy of Hef's sextu-plets, hot girls on the street who lust after them, and when it comes to female anatomy, much more about the hunt and chase than body parts. Partly, it's that men and women stretch the truth about different things. Some men tend to lie about cheating, stealing, and sex; the things that make them feel powerful and important. Some women lie about food, money, and orgasms; the things that make them feel secure and what they think others want to hear.

   So when it comes to sex and playing the field, guys love to talk about quantity. If they bring up specific girls, chances are they're playing around and not interested in anything deep and meaningful. Or at least, meaningful.

What does he say about you after the first date? It depends on how he views his date with you, and how ingrained the Madonna and Whore Complex is with him. Sadly, it's still ingrained pretty heavily in society. Guys don't talk about the girl they want as wife and mother to their kids. But they laugh and joke about the loose girl at the bar who's kind of slutty and fun. You should know that gay guys take the straight man bravado with a huge lump of salt. We know that when he's bragging about how into him you are, he's spinning more than we do in the bicycle class. If half of it is true, we'd be surprised.

2. *When He Doesn't Talk About His Dates, Then He Either Cares a Lot or Not at All.* There's a huge gap in how women and men view announcing that they're dating someone new. As Cathy says, "I couldn't figure out why the guy I'd been dating for months hadn't told any of his friends about me. We were having a hot time. I thought he'd brag up and down. I asked, 'Are you embarrassed of me?' He was truly surprised. I tell you every dirty detail, analyzing what it all means, blow by blow, if you will. He tells his friends nothing. Why?"

Here's the deal. It's all about freedom. For some men, the worst thing you can do is take away freedom. If he tells people about you, or introduces you to his friends, then you become part of the equation. He knows you are likeable and his friends would invite you places and ask about you. Announcing that he's dating you is a much bigger deal for him. What would be easy for you to handle feels overwhelming to him.

3. *There's Jock Itch and There's Also the Seven-Year Itch.* You tell me that no relationship is perfect, yet still you wish your straight man would show his softer side. I am not sure you really want that, but maybe you want more common ground between you. Meanwhile, he's talking with his friends about how he wishes you'd lose the sweatpants and rediscover the miniskirt and f***-me pumps he first fancied you in, when you were polished and painted a lot more than you are these days. He doesn't want more common ground. He wants more distinction. The guys joke about it, but is there some truth there? The point is that both of you wish the other would occasionally shake it up.

4. *Inquiring Minds Want to Know—What's up with the Bathroom Two-at-a-Time Routine?* Two by two, women still trudge off to the ladies room together. I know it's socially acceptable, but in these enlightened times of less stereotypical sex roles, guys really don't get it. One straight guy told me that he "doesn't trust when girls go to the bathroom together. It just seems like they want to gossip. They can't be up to any good."

5. *Please, No More "Am I Fat?" Questions.* Of course, questions like "Does my butt look fat in this?" have less to do with whether you've gained weight than they

do with confidence. Guys like confident women. Lack of confidence is a big turnoff. Look around. Guys are hot for girls with luscious, full, and adult female bodies, as opposed to the "Nadia Comenici at thirteen years old" waif ideal espoused by fashion magazines. If guys like curves, then why don't you? The answer probably has more to do with the "Anna Wintour Skinny Vogue Bitch" complex than anything else. Or in simpler terms, the Madison Avenue advertising ideal, which still shows women wearing size zero. How much of men's "modelizer" behavior is about attraction to confidence? Staying in shape is important, but learn to like your curves so that you have confidence in front of your guy.

6. *Men Smell Desperation Like Dogs Smell Fear.* Guys hate the "desperate, clingy thing," as one of them referred to it. It's especially grating early on in a relationship. Not only is it unattractive, but also men sense (correctly, I think) that the desperation isn't really about them. It's about the woman's insecurity. Without getting too Freudian, if a woman is that desperate, it means she wants a man, any man. It's deeply unflattering to a straight man to think a woman sees him only as "straight man," not as a real person. Of course, he'd never articulate that to you. Are you kidding?

7. *A Glance Is Worth a Thousand Words.* Do straight men compare and check each other out? Yes. All men compare, usually silently. We follow rules of silence (or at least minimal conversation) when at the urinals. Unlike

women, we don't sit in adjoining bathroom stalls chatting about our day. We communicate. But 80 percent of all communication is nonverbal. In some ways, the locker room is a perfect example of that. As Ted, a straight guy at the gym, told me, "Girls talk. With guys, the eyes do all the work. It's silent comparing. You won't hear us talking about it later."

8. *Straight Men Have No Interest in Being Your Gay Boyfriend*. I'd breathe a huge sigh of relief on this one. Why would you want them to be your gay boyfriend anyway? They don't want to be that guy, and often talk about the fine line between being sensitive and being a certified, 100 percent proof homosexual. Thirty-three-year-old gym buddy Jimmy told me, "Women say that they want a sensitive, expressive, sweet, and nonthreatening man. Yeah, they want that at the specific time they want that. But not at other times. They want you to be a heterosexual guy with blatant hetero male traits, too. If you are just all of those sweet traits, they just think you're gay and dismiss you. Nothing against gay guys." I love it when straight guys end a conversation with me that way. Nothing against you either, Jimmy. Finally, they don't readily admit it, but straight guys are curious about your relationship with your gay friend. What is it that you get so excited about sharing with us? Ah, mystery. Let them wonder.

9. *Men Prefer Quantity over Quality*. "Sex is like pizza. Even when it's bad, it's good," said Vince, twenty-nine-year-old production director in New York. What

I learned from Vince and a few others is that guys aren't as obsessed with mind-blowing sex, i.e. quality, as they are with quantity. Of course, everybody wants mind-blowing sex, but when push comes to shove, women I've interviewed prefer quality to quantity. A few straight guys I know want to kick Sting's ass for saying he made love for eight solid hours through some mysterious tantric sex rituals. Sting later modified his statement, claiming that the eight hours included dinner and a movie. I always felt he made the disclaimer under threats from some underground militant straight guy group.

10. *They Don't Have the Venting Thing Down at All.* You'd think straight guys would learn that women need to vent about problems, and not get them fixed. Sorry, they're not there yet. They're slowly grasping the concept, but it's still reflexive to be the emotional handyman. I know, I know. You've told me a million times. Women want their guy to listen, so why does the guy insist on giving advice *as if he isn't really listening?*

6

DO YOU SUFFER FROM MALE PATTERN DYSFUNCTION?

How to break the cycle before you wind up married to your father's worst traits.

"I was on a date and it hit me. All of a sudden, I looked at Aaron and realized I was looking into the eyes of my father. I should have run right there and then. Instead, I married him." Jenny, thirty-five, described what should have been her happiest day with all the enthusiasm of someone headed to jail. In her case, she might say she already was in jail.

If you are a woman, the inevitability of being attracted to a man who embodies the worst traits of your father is as assured as death and taxes.

Melissa, a thirty-two-year-old career counselor, has helped innumerable women and men find better jobs, but she found herself soul searching one day about her marriage. Her husband was like her dad in some ways. Whenever she'd try to discuss important life matters like children, work issues, or finances, he made jokes, like Dad did. He clearly didn't take her seriously.

I asked her, "Is this really what you want?" She later told me it was the best advice she's ever received, though on the surface it seems like such as simple question. But when you are used to being treated a certain way, you develop a blind spot. As her friend, it was much more effective to ask her what she wanted than to make her decisions for her. After all, she was considering leaving a man who didn't take her seriously. Why would she accept listening to a friend who preached?

It's not a question of *if* you'll meet such a man. It's a question of *when*. And your chances exponentially increase if your relationship with your father leaves a lot to be desired. A bumper sticker I saw recently articulated, "The trouble with some women is they get all excited about nothing, and then they marry him." Can you change the type of man who attracts you? Is ending up with Bad Dad Part Deux a foregone conclusion? Having met my girlfriends' fathers and dates, I see the similarities, good and bad. As a man, I have insight into male behavior, so I know what to warn you about. As your gay best friend, I'll lift the veil we all wear during the initial stages of new romance.

Somehow, a man marrying a girl who reminds him of dear old Mom doesn't carry as much negative emotional baggage as the girl who mates with the guy who's the spitting image of Papa. Of course, there's always the chance that a girl will fall into the mama's boy trap, in which terrifying mom is on speed dial, and son slowly turns into a modern day version of Norman Bates. But more likely, a man who likes his mother and wants a woman like her respects women.

With women, the daddy factor seems to fall into two distinct camps, neither good.

OPTION A: Dad was a saint, she's a daddy's girl, and every potential Mr. Right is a complete disappointment. This is called "Little Princess Syndrome" (LPS), and invariably the women I have met who have LPS face a lifetime of overly high expectations that will never be met by a living, breathing, and mortal man.

OPTION B: Dad was a distant, self-centered SOB (or some variation thereof), and she's inextricably drawn to a junior version of him. I am naturally protective of you, as a brother would be, in addition to having essential nonfamilial distance and the right set of chromosomes. These give me a superhero's laser-like vision to assess the daddy quotient in your relationship.

Of course, the extremes of both options A and B make your gay boyfriend say "Ew!" Neither is pretty. Both of these options require new thinking of the old daddy issue.

For most girls, the first male influence is your dad. You grew up in his world with his behaviors, lifestyle, and views. Not to get too Freudian, but obviously Dad's influence set the starting point for your subsequent relationships with men. As the song goes, "It's not where you start, it's where you finish." And I want you to finish happy, with the right guy by your side.

When Sarah, a thirty-year-old high-tech businesswoman, was dating a cocky guy who treated her badly, I spoke up. She was feeling miserable and out of control. "It doesn't matter how you learned to reward bad behavior in men, but when are you going to stop it?" I asked. This particular "man-boy" (according to my emotional maturity calculations, he was twenty-seven going on six) had just told his pal,

"I'm going to wait a few days before I call Sarah, and let her sweat it a bit." She spent time thinking about her relationship with her quiet and puritanical dad that led her to expect little from men. Afterwards, she cut man-boy off and didn't return his call when he finally rang her a week later. Sarah let him sweat it out. Instead of calling him back, she went out and met the cool guy she is still seeing.

There's a myth that women don't have control over the men they love. I don't believe it. They absolutely do. I fault the soulmate theory of relationships, the one that states that there's only one man for every woman, and your job is to find him and then keep him at all costs. Even Meg Ryan, queen of those types of romantic comedy films, admitted in a recent interview that a few of her movies perpetuated this unhelpful myth.

"I thought the dad connection was an absurd cliché," says Paula. "It is a cliché but there's truth in it. My father is self-absorbed. All the men I dated before I started making the dad connection to my romantic life were similarly self-absorbed. Now I think that the absurd cliché is you have no choice in love." Fate won't be nearly as cruel as you'll be to yourself if you don't examine the past in order to break the cycle.

Don't do it just for yourself. Do the daughters or nieces you'll have a huge favor and break the cycle now. Though your gay boyfriend's advice will serve as a constant reminder, nothing is as effective as the example of someone who's really made the change. So here's how to make sure Mr. Right doesn't end being Bad Daddy in sheep's clothing:

1. *Knowing Your Roots Doesn't Just Apply to Your Hair.* Really examine your relationship (or lack thereof) with

your father. What was positive about it for you? What was not so positive? Write down the traits you want in a man and how they correspond with your father's traits. The written word is sometimes more powerful than a fleeting thought. When you see on paper that your dad's numero uno trait was self-absorption, which happens to be the same trait of all the men in your life, maybe it's time to make that your red flag in any new relationship.

2. *Avoid Stockholm Syndrome.* In 1973, four Swedes held in a bank vault for six days during a robbery became attached to their captors, a phenomenon dubbed the Stockholm Syndrome. According to psychologists, the abused bond to their abusers as a way to avoid more trouble. What does this mean for your relationships with men? In layman's terms, it can run the gamut from putting up with too much crap to allowing a man to treat you poorly because it's what you are used to. If you had or have a father who didn't treat you so well, and fear you might be exhibiting signs of Stockholm Syndrome in your relationships with men, the first step to breaking free is getting out of denial. That's where I come in. When it comes to men who don't treat you as well as they should, I take no prisoners, and neither should you. Lock them out of your life.

3. *Create Your Own Standards.* It's good to have standards, lines in the sand that you draw for reasonable behavior. The key word, of course, is reasonable. In a romantic relationship, "reasonable" isn't always a twist on the old Golden Rule of others doing unto you as you do

unto them. Men and women act differently in some ways. That's to be expected. For example, women like to vent without having their problems fixed more than men do. That doesn't make either side wrong, it's just important to understand so you can manage it. That's different than lack of standards. When I asked Paula about her deal breakers in a romantic relationship, she said, "When I was dating a lot, I hate to admit it, but I don't think I had any." Often women are unflinchingly loyal to their fathers and this translates to romantic relationships with men. Unless he's missing teeth, living with Mom in a doublewide trailer, and his car is permanently at the shop, there are some women who'd still give him the benefit of the obvious, well-reasoned doubt. But love isn't blind, and loyalty isn't either.

4. *Earth to Princess, It's a Two-Way Street.* On the other hand, if you idolized your father, who treated you like a princess, be careful not to set unreachable standards for every man you meet. Your highness, that's a one-way ticket to the land of disappointment (a not-so-amusement-oriented park I have visited a few times myself). It's good to hold all the men accountable for treating you well. But remember that a relationship is a two-way street. Treat each other like royalty to ensure balance.

5. *Cut Your Losses.* Sadly, many of the women who realized they were in a relationship with men who embodied their father's worst traits were well into it before they had the shocking realization. Hindsight is always 20-20, isn't it? But no matter how awful that moment of

realization is, you can do something about it. As much as we all like to think that leopards change their spots, it's rare that they do. I'd put a timeline on trying to reestablish healthier relationship dynamics. If at the end of the evaluation period (which can involve heart-to-heart talks, counseling, and, of course, advice and input from your gay boyfriend) you are still staring Bad Daddy Jr. in the face, then you need to ask yourself the old Ann Landers question: "Would my life be better with or without him?" If it's the latter, cut your losses and leave the worst of Daddy behind.

Five Simple Rules for Avoiding a Man with Your Father's Worst Traits

1. Never date a man who calls you "baby" on the first date.

2. Ask your closest friends who'd know: "Does he remind you of my dad in any way?" Even if the two men are similar in healthy ways, you need objective viewpoints.

3. Never date a man who thinks the term "loaded dishwasher" refers to his drunk wife.

4. Never have sex with anybody who has more problems than you do.

5. Run from the house if your father meets your awful, beer-swigging, rude, disrespectful boyfriend for the first time and says, "That's my kind of guy."

7

KEEPING YOUR ROMANTIC PIPELINE FULL OF MEN

Keep throwing them against the wall until one of them sticks, and other methods.

Marcie, twenty-seven, cute, and maybe a little spoiled by her wealthy dad, sits in her expensive Los Angeles rental and contemplates dating. "I don't meet men, and I am not about to hang out in bars to meet guys. That is just so pathetic."

Maybe, but I made the case to her that being in your twenties, living in Los Angeles as a single woman who stays in every night except for the occasional night out with the girls and gays, could be considered equally pathetic. God knows, gay men sometimes exhibit traits that one could call pathetic. Consuming copious amounts of drugs named after women during all-night benders at dance clubs (Tina or Connie, anyone?) is a peculiarity that comes to mind. But staying inside like shut-ins because we're worried about what people might think if we hang out with friends in bars isn't one of them. Why should it be one of yours either? Get over the "good girls don't go out and howl" mindset. Leave the single solitude to cloistered nuns. This is life, not Catholic school.

"Don't sit back passively waiting. And don't put all your eggs in one man's basket, so to speak," I told Marcie. "You've got to think of men as a continuous stream of possibilities that you consider until you choose to go ashore with one of them. The key phrases are 'best option' and 'you choose.' Men are like spaghetti noodles. Throw them against the wall until one of them sticks. They are like darts. Keep playing until you hit the bulls-eye."

There are many options for meeting men these days (see chapter 2 for my list). I don't want you sitting at home alone watching a weekend movie marathon unless the films star Hugh Jackman (in which case, I might join you). With all the options, why wait for love to come knocking? You might be waiting a really long time.

As Jamie told me, "Having a gay man to talk to about dating is so helpful because he isn't going to sit around waiting for dates to happen. He has no problems going out and getting what he wants, which inspires me. He knows what men are thinking when they like someone (and what they do when they lose interest). He also knows what's worked and not worked in the past for himself when it comes to snagging a man, and can share those techniques. Straight male friends know only what works for snagging women (though often they don't even have a clue about that!). Besides, they're not always honest about what they want from a woman or a relationship when you ask them."

"You have to have a herd, and that means five at any

time," says Brian, gay boyfriend to several women in Washington. "You have to tame the herd, adjust for comings and goings, and don't neglect the herd. One might be a prospect, one might be a hot fling, another might be relationship-material, others might be 'longshots,' 'newbies,' and 'undetermined status.'

Myreah Moore's book *Date Like a Man* says you need a "pair and a spare," which is basically a slightly smaller version of the herd, if you find the idea of one intimidating. But if you want to date like a gay man, then you need a herd.

Not only does a herd help keep you calm as you emotionally toggle between different guys, it's also a good way to fight the Social A.D.D. that is rampant in metropolitan areas. Singles in urban areas get used to life on the hamster wheel. When it works, then life seems spontaneous, fun, and exciting. There's a new friend, party, and man right around the next corner. But the downside is what I call Social A.D.D, a condition caused by too many options, especially when it comes to dating. It's particularly dangerous for straight men in urban environments. Women seem to have the ability (maturity?) to overcome the downsides of Social A.D.D. But even in the best and calmest of situations, men have zero attention spans. Put them into the social whirl of a metropolis, and watch their heads spin like Linda Blair's in *The Exorcist*. The distraction doesn't even have to be something equal or better. As long as it's different, the men are off and running from ride to ride at the amusement park. "The roller coaster was the best! It's my favorite! Oh, look! There's the water slide. That's my favorite now!" I have seen much fallout from this behavior. After dates that both parties agreed were awesome, the men disappear. It's not even a long story. It's a short story that repeats. Rachel calls these poor Social A.D.D.–afflicted men, "The League of Human Vanishers."

Here's what gay men and gamblers have understood for years: dating is a numbers game. You have to play to win. When you fish, you go where the fish are. It can be exciting to experiment with visiting new places or trying new approaches. But don't do anything too contrived. It could backfire, like it did on poor twenty-six-year-old Laura. "I had the biggest crush on my neighbor's best friend. I found out he loved camping so I made a point of telling him at a party how much I just loved camping. I'd never been camping before. To make a long story short, we dated for a couple of months, and it came time to pay the piper for my lie. He was so excited as we left for our first camping trip. He kept telling me how glad he was to have found a girl to share his favorite activity. I felt like such a loser. I was miserable. I could only fake it for so long. He ended up really disappointed."

You see, it's a common male misconception that the only thing women fake is sex. Wrong. Women like Laura fake hobbies, too. But it backfires.

With that one caveat in mind, here's what you must keep in mind as you go fishing where the "fish" are, and, hopefully, keep your pipeline full of fabulous catches:

1. *Don't Be a Mouse Potato.* What's a mouse potato? It's the online, wired generation's answer to the couch potato. You're not going to find a great guy staring at your computer screen. Online personals and chat

rooms are perfectly acceptable ways to meet men (although finding a guy in a cyber chat room who wants to meet you for more than a sex date is rare!). But you must get out there "live and in person," too. To paraphrase an old expression, "Don't hide your light behind your screen saver."

2. *Run with a Pack*. Amy says, "I am all for girl power in numbers when it comes to meeting men. We get a little more dressed up, reinforce the 'we've got it!' attitude with each other before we go, and then roll out to the clubs and restaurants in a pack of four or more. You can't believe the attention from men that four women or more get when they're out having fun. We are a pack of confident, fun women (that night, at least) and the energy is magnetic. It only works when it's just women. Add a guy to the mix and it spoils it."

3. *Don't Falsely Advertise*. Some gay men falsely advertise by claiming to want a relationship when, in fact, they want a relationship as much as a bar rash. Women tend to falsely advertise by pretending they're up for a meaningless, cheap affair. So be clear about what you really want and honestly convey that on and offline. Dating dissatisfaction is often the result of misleading advertising; one or both people not telling the truth about the level of dating each wants.

4. *Stay Casual Early On*. Straight men like an initially casual approach. Just like you've had your share of flakes, straight men on the dating track have had their share of

hysterical women who jumped the gun. As my straight friend Rich put it, "You have to be careful. My buddy met a girl two weeks ago and has been debating how to approach her ever since. He's worried about asking her out on a 'pressured' date. The last time he did, the girl misread his intentions and is still lobbing emotionally charged voice mail grenades into his camp. He withdrew from dating completely for a few months. Asking her out for a drink sounds too lame, dinner sounds too formal. He planned to ask her out for drinks when they can meet up with mutual friends afterwards. He's still waiting for his pals to come up with a suitable night. I (almost) felt sorry for him."

5. *Tend Your Herd*. It's a noble thing to be a one-man woman. If you are one, then this is especially important for you. As a one-man woman, you'll likely put all your eggs in one man's basket. But when you are dating, with no committed relationship on the immediate horizon, then consider the benefits of a herd. You might have your opinions on who among your herd is likely to break out and win your heart, but a man has to earn that special placement in the herd. He doesn't get that status just because you have "a feeling." I always say that feelings are free, have as many of them as you want. But be careful which ones you act upon. Pay attention to the men in your herd and cultivate them slowly. You might be surprised when the tortoise of the group overtakes the hare.

6. *Get Another Horse*. Remember the old saying that "When you fall off a horse, get back on," for fear that

you'll be too scared to at a later date. Apply it to dating. "Go get another one and get back on the horse," is the advice Rachel appreciated most from her friend Mark.

7. *Flirting Is a Muscle.* Would you be surprised if your muscles atrophied after months of skipping the gym? So don't be surprised when, after a long dry spell with guys, your flirting skills leave a lot to be desired. Flirting is a muscle. You must exercise your muscles. Don't wait until you are in a situation with a potentially hot prospect to suddenly test your strength. Practice along the way. You'll lose nothing and probably have a much better time if you flirt more. Flirting isn't a contract. Women sometimes forget this. It actually serves many purposes, in addition to making the object of your desire get the point. It makes people feel attractive and it connects you in a more sensual way to the moment.

8. *Don't Invest Too Early.* There's an old saying about gambling: you shouldn't bet what you can't afford to lose. Stockbrokers and Wall Street analysts are always trying to judge market timing for investing. Follow the rules of investing when you're dating a new man. Don't invest too soon. Get more information before you make a commitment. Nothing is 100 percent foolproof, but what's the reasonable certainty given various key market factors?

8

INVESTIGATING A
NEW MAN

Ms. Sherlock and her gay Watson offer simple
yet effective ways to find out what you need
to know . . . before you get too involved.

Sometimes it pays to have a sibling in law enforcement. For
nothing more than a little something extra in the gift bag at
holiday time, you can put on Sherlock Holmes's cap quickly
and easily. In no time, you can uncover a potential suitor's
criminal record, credit history, investment records, recent
Internet site hits, and video rental selections. Why go to all
the trouble? The main reason is that in today's uncertain
world, a girl can't be too careful. A secondary benefit is that
snooping is a total guilty pleasure.

But for those of you who, unlike me, have no siblings
working the right side of the law, there are still plenty of options for you to evaluate a potential mate. The last thing your
gay best friend wants to deal with is you ditched at the altar
on your wedding day, mascara streaming down your cheeks

like Tammy Faye Baker, cursing God because Mr. Wonderful ran off with your life savings.

Mutual friends introduce few couples these days. It's sad but true. Arranged marriages are frowned upon in the U.S., unless you're on a Fox reality TV show. So you are left with no choice but to find the man of your dreams on your own. That's only half of the daunting task. The other half is making sure he's a decent man, with nothing more outstanding than a stack of parking tickets.

In addition to the obvious checks, such as meeting his family and friends after a reasonable period of dating, you need to be aware of other options for making sure Mr. Right isn't also "Mr. Top Ten Most Wanted" by the FBI.

Since gay men rarely have the usual posse of family, friends, and large social network on hand to evaluate potential mates, we've had to take investigative matters into our own hands. Our families don't tend to be overprotective of us when it comes to our relationships. Most of us haven't been married so we've missed prewedding counseling, which at least provides a forum for objective evaluation. So we learn early on to evaluate other men. Gay men know all too well that men's appearances can be deceiving. Just as women sometimes sense other women's secrets, men often have a way of seeing the truth about other men.

"Gay guys have a sixth sense, I am convinced of it. They have always been on target for me when it comes to men. My coworkers, including a few gay men, go out together socially after work. James, one of the gay guys, always looks out for me when it comes to potential suitors. He is an expert at the 'two-second size-up.' He analyzes the guy I am interested in, and he's usually on target," says Kristy, a thirty-four-year-old manager in Virginia.

Gay men grow up in an unsafe world and have to be more aware of their surroundings. Concerned about exposing ourselves, some of us develop a finely tuned ability to assess people's motivations. It gives us an observer's eye.

If our eyes aren't enough, thank God for the power of the Internet. As resourceful Washington paralegal Jim told me, "My dad is a lawyer and I used his firm to check out my friend Lisa's date. The firm has access to public records as well as several search engines. It turns out the guy was clean. She was relieved and grateful. It was all in a day's work."

It's sad that we resort to what seem like John Grisham plotlines to evaluate prospects. But a lot of things are sadder. In the eighteenth century, a man could be hauled off to jail for misrepresenting himself, his intentions or his background to a woman. Can't you picture the 18th century woman scorned? She hurls herself onto her day bed, a jar of smelling salts in her trembling hand, and sighs, "I have the vapors!" to no one in particular before she passes out from shock. Today you don't have to wait to be scorned. Your motto should be: "A girl has the right to know!" It applies to so many situations.

Let's consider the following options as we explore the burgeoning world of friendly networking, simple research and personal history checks you can do on potential mates. Think about what kinds of information you'll want to see—in black and white—before you merge hearts, lives, friends, family, real estate, and finances.

1. *You've Got to Have Friends.* Friends and referrals are the tried and true way to get a reference on a prospect. Unfortunately, they're rare in today's fend-for-yourself society. It makes you long for the days of arranged marriages, doesn't it? Well, you long for the *fantasy* arranged marriage, where the man is fun, smart, handsome, rich, daddy's tiger in the bedroom and mommy's lamb when it comes to household chores. How many arranged marriages ever fulfilled that fantasy? Not many, I'd guess. Instead, tap into the friends of friends network as much as you can. Help each other sort the wheat from the chaff when it comes to guys. As Cathleen said after a bad relationship ended, "If I had asked people who knew the guy a few more questions earlier on, I probably would not have dated him. Or, at least, I would not have been surprised." Twenty-six-year-old entrepreneur Suzanne was even more direct. She tracked her man's whereabouts by making friends with his female colleague and getting access to his schedule.

2. *Make Friends with Straight Boys!* Straight guys will often give you the backstory on their friend. But the trick is to avoid directly asking about the guy's potential. Make your queries as casual as possible, so his friends will be distracted and just start talking. Guys love to compare, so ask questions that subtly make his friends compare him to them in the areas of girls, nightlife, habits, and interests. Susan, twenty-eight-year-old financial planner from Maryland, has this down. "I was interested in

a neighbor named Todd who had two housemates. I ran into one of the housemates as he washed his car, started a conversation, and asked him who partied the most in his house, that sort of thing. Very friendly, easygoing banter. As he hosed the car down, he sang like a canary, as they say on *The Sopranos*. I learned that Todd was the quiet one who came home from parties early, wasn't as wild and was looking for a relationship but was shyer around girls. Bingo."

3. *Tap Into the Gay Network.* We are everywhere. Tap into the gay network and you are more plugged in than P. Diddy at the Grammy's. "I used to call my friend John 'The Lookout,'" says twenty-nine-year-old Deb. "We worked together but on different floors. I was smitten with Paul, who worked a few offices down from John. We had a simmering flirtation but both of us were recently out of relationships. We needed a spark to move us from simmer to boil. John kept track of Paul's comings and goings, so I knew optimal times to walk by, such as when Paul was hanging out talking with other coworkers, in a really good mood, or really busy."

4. *But Don't Tap Us Out.* Though we love you and will do anything for you, please don't put us in jeopardy. For example, Lilly, a thirty-three-year-old real estate broker from Ohio, was seized by desperation so she dialed for help. "My gay best friend Jack is a loan officer with a bank and would run credit checks on prospects for me, on a very selective basis of course," said Lilly. "I

know, I know. It was absolutely immoral, but it saved me from at least one deadbeat. One guy was in default of at least three loans, and had racked up over $50,000 in credit-card debt. As a successful businesswomen, I felt like he had to be looking at me as his meal ticket." It all worked out, but Jack can't pull too many of those reports without getting caught by the Feds.

5. *Dialing for the Real 411*. It's a new information age, and you can't rely on stalking by phone anymore. "I've called him from phones not my own. In these days of caller ID, you have to be much more clever than before," says Jackie, a thirty-year-old educator from Florida. Want to play telephone detective to check on his whereabouts? Call from a different number. I am ashamed to admit (OK, not really) that, as a favor for my friend Rachel, I called a man named Brandon on his cell phone. He and Rachel had dated, but he'd stopped returning calls. She wanted to know if he was still alive but didn't want to call him anymore.

6. *To Cruise a Thief*. Your gay friend can act as your beard while you safely scope out the guys. Ever play the, "Is he or isn't he?" game when you and your gay friend are out in public? Hopefully you'll have a better experience than David and Carol. There's a romantic cat-and-mouse thriller called *To Catch a Thief*, but *To Cruise a Thief* would be more like it for them. "We were shopping at an office supply store, checking out the same guy. Just as we looked at each other and gave a big wink and thumbs up, our prospect stole something and ran out of the store.

This made us realize we both had questionable taste in men. I am happy to say that our tastes have since improved. But now we don't spend quite as much time checking out men. Instead, we quickly mutter under our breaths, "Your team or my team?" and keep walking.

7. *Brush, Floss, and Google Every Day.* Jump on the Google bandwagon and see what you find when you type his name and any relevant identifiers (school, job, or major hobbies) into the search box. It's easy to get information on him, but since many names are common, just make sure you have the right guy. During my interviews, I met a women who Googled a man she'd met seconds earlier at a bar by typing his name into her web-enabled PDA. Now that's instant gratification! If for some reason you don't have time to do it yourself, call one of your gay male friends like Carol did. "I was waiting for a blind date and called my gay friend who did a web search on him. 'What's his name?' he asked. 'Ponzi Smith,' I said. Within seconds, he yelled out 'Ponzi Smith?!! He's a complete crook.' " Apparently there were news reports of how he'd scammed people for money. The irony wasn't lost on Carol, who noted, "Though I overlooked his name at first, it turns out there was truth in this advertising."

8. *Do a Dating IPO and Go Public.* For your dating pre-screen check, do you need more information than free web sites can provide? Try buying a public record report. They start as low as $9.95 from sites such as Yahoo's B-2-B portal.

9. *Don't Forget Weblogs.* The say that criminals always want to get caught. It's certainly true for idiots, too. Jean, a twenty-nine-year-old high-tech consultant from Maryland, was exhausted from her eighty-hour-a-week job when she met twenty-nine-year-old web developer Stan. It was a match made in high-tech heaven, or so Jean thought until she did a web search on Stan. She found Stan's weblog, which described in detail his innermost thoughts and daily plans. Jean got the rare opportunity to read what Stan wrote about her after their dates. One of the logs included, "Jean is pretty cool but, dudes, there's no way I am slowing down the chick chase. I make sure to act totally interested in her. She has no idea that I am such a horndog. Gotta play to win, bros!" Jean had the rare opportunity to deeply explore the shallow recesses of the immature straight male's mind, laid out for her in glorious black-and-white type. I have always said that everything you need to learn about a guy you can learn in the first five minutes. Before, it meant you asked the right questions. Now all you have to do is a quick web search.

10. America's Most Wanted *is Must See TV for a Single Girl.* Add John Walsh's show *America's Most Wanted* to your list of essential reality TV viewing, right up there with *The Bachelor/Bachelorette* dating show. Does your date have that wild-eyed, skittish look, like a trapped animal desperately seeking safety? Granted, you have to be really bad to make the top ten list, so maybe you won't see him on TV. But think Animal

Planet and remember this: when you suspect he's a weasel, ferret out the truth.

11. *Learn from Gay Men.* It's no secret that many gay men tend to hook up fairly proficiently. Some women envy a gay guy's freedom to shamelessly find other gay guys. Men don't have societal pressure to passively wait. What many women don't realize is that there's an inverse correlation between how quickly gay men date and how slowly we get into real relationships. We may meet fast, but the real relationships tend to build slowly. We are a little hesitant to get intertwined and that's a good thing. We are protective of our careers, finances, and what can be time-consuming romances. You should be, too.

9

STALKING BEHAVIOR

Sending him a long e-mail when he doesn't call you immediately after the second date, and other behaviors that require my intervention.

Why is it that some women don't know the difference be-tween a sunny postdate follow up phone call and a three-page stalking e-mail?

"Stalk" is defined as "to follow or observe [a person] per-sistently, especially out of obsession or derangement. To move threateningly or menacingly. To track prey or quarry. See stalked, stalking, stalks."

It's illegal in some states. That means I can no longer stand by and risk being your accomplice as you hunt down your latest romantic obsession. One thing I've noticed with women is how you have different needs for boundaries in a relationship, especially a burgeoning one. As a gay man, I understand a straight man's need for independence, free-dom, and space. For example, when in doubt, women want to talk. When in doubt, men don't.

Poor thirty-four-year-old Liz! She'd been seeing Anthony for six months and was troubled by his unwillingness to introduce her to his friends despite the fact that they were having a great time together. As Liz put it, "Here I am telling you every dirty detail of this romance, analyzing what it all means, blow-by-blow, uh, if you will. And when I asked Anthony if he's told anyone about our dalliance, he said, 'No—but I will.' Ugh! I have had it!"

But why is she so upset? Liz will readily admit she didn't want a committed relationship any more than Anthony did. In fact, they talked about it and agreed that the romance they had was perfect for them at this time in their lives. Somewhere along the line she had forgotten this and had decided to confront him. I quickly assessed Anthony's profile: job in jeopardy, recent divorce, and five-year-old son. Anthony's biggest fear is someone taking away what little freedom he has left. Men understand this. As I told Liz, "The minute he introduces you to his friends or family, you become part of the whole equation. Next thing he knows, he's being asked how you are in every conversation. You become part of the furniture, and part of the pressure he feels if his family wants him to settle down again." When in doubt, women talk more and men talk less. It seems simple, but when you are a girl whose pride is on the line, maybe it's hard to see that, in some instances, a guy's behavior toward you has more to do with him than you. Luckily I was able to stop Liz from driving to Anthony's house at midnight, banging on the door like a madwoman, and venting her fury. All it took was a little old-fashioned gay ingenuity, sound male logic, and, of course, slashing her tires so she couldn't drive.

I want you to see how behavior that you think should increase communication often has the opposite effect on men. Learn it before it drives you to the point of no return.

Jenny and Tim, twentysomethings from Boston, met through friends and went on a fun date, followed a stroll by the Charles River in the moonlight. At the end of the night, in a moment of unbridled enthusiasm, they exchanged all telephone numbers—work, home, and cell. Exchanging all telephone numbers is unquestionably a sign that someone wants to be more accessible to you. It's like telling someone, "I'll be here, or here, or even here, if you want to find me anytime." I think we do this a little too quickly. There's often "morning-after remorse" following such a comprehensive number exchange. That probably explains the chilly reception Jenny got when she called Tim at work the next day. On some level, despite being invited in, she invaded his world. Remember the *Seinfeld* episode about Independent George vs. Relationship George? (Okay, George Costanza is hardly anyone's choice for a dating prospect, but there's a point coming.) Poor George felt suffocated by his date and poured his concern out to Jerry. The conversation went something like this:

> "You have no idea of the magnitude of this thing. If she is allowed to infiltrate this world then George Costanza as you know him ceases to exist. You see, right now I have Relationship George. But there is also Independent George. That's the George you know, the George you grew up with ... Movie George, Coffee Shop George, Liar George, Bawdy George."

"I love that George."

"Me too, and he's dying. If Relationship George walks through this door, he will kill Independent George. A George divided against itself cannot stand!"

The point is that for some guys, a call at work is what you get from your wife or girlfriend, not the girl you went out with last night. Men are much more compartmentalized than women and calling him at work might be invading a compartment he's not ready to have invaded yet. So even if the jackass gives you his work number, and you take it as an invitation, don't necessarily ring him up right away.

Rachel calls the men who just disappear without a trace after, by all normal accounts, you've had a good time with them "The League of Male Vanishers." There are a million reasons why a guy would be part of that league, most of them having nothing to do with you and everything to do with him and his maturity levels.

Of course, the worst and most severe threat to a guy's independence is the work romance. It starts off especially exciting if your long-term crush on a guy is finally realized. The all-consuming wait is over! A few boring days at work can make the cute guy down the hall look that much more exciting in comparison. Even in the best of circumstances, you will see him every day and night. That's not usually a good thing as you chart the scary, rocky, "one step forward, one step back" course to a relationship. The risks usually outweigh the benefits. My office romance went south faster than Sherman and his tanks. If the romance doesn't work out, plotting your every trip to the water cooler to avoid him is no emotional picnic.

Of course, maintaining the balance of independence and connection in a romance works both ways. I know you hate certain male behaviors such as the "I'll call you" game, followed by no call and the full gallop of intimacy, followed by his pulling back the reins. On the other hand, when the guy is like a little gnat hanging around you all the time, you hate that as much as a guy hates feeling stalked by a girl. "If I don't like the guy, I hate the 'instant intimacy' thing they try to create sometimes," said thirty-five-year-old hotel manager Liz. "You know the type. One date and he's all over you like you've been dating for six months."

Worse is the infamous "Guy Who Won't Leave," says twenty-nine-year-old Carrie. "He just assumes I've been waiting for him all my life. It's annoying. If he gets too familiar too soon, like plopping himself down on the sofa, grabbing a beer and the remote control, and clicking away on one of our first dates, he is so over. I feel like saying, 'This isn't a *Honeymooners* rerun on TV Land, my friend. Get your potato ass off my couch.' I have this instant flash forward to him glued to my couch and me totally trapped."

The answer on both sides is to follow this dating rule. Don't challenge a man's independence too soon, just as you don't want some lamprey of a guy latching onto you prematurely, either.

Invading his space works in your favor if you want to dump the guy but feel bad about it. "The tactic I'm considering for getting rid of Tony is to act super-clingy. I'm going to call daily and whisper hoo-hah like, 'P.S. I really like you.' If I just tell him I'll be avoiding him from now on, it'll take too much energy. I mean that's punishment but he is the one who's stood me up and kept me hanging, so it seems that the punishment should fit the crime."

When it comes to postdate behavior, it's time to take the bull by the horns (or the cow by the ears, as it were) and lay down the law. The following guidelines will help you clarify the man-woman dating communication struggles and distinguish acceptable vs. prison-worthy behavior.

1. *Lighten Up.* Of course, that's easy to say and harder to do, especially if you've just come home from a thrilling, fun date with a man who gets all of your senses percolating. Enjoy your enthusiasm until it sends your expectations into overdrive. As law student Jackie says, "Men's idiosyncrasies that confuse women are easy for gay guys to understand." Men are strange, dating is quirky, and there could be a hundred reasons why it will or won't work out. It's not your job to project the future with this guy. That will take care of itself. But the future won't stand a chance if you are too overbearing.

2. *Leave the Stakeouts to the Cops.* Stakeouts don't always work. Twenty-two-year-old Donna had been dating a guy for a few months, and decided to find out if he was seeing anyone else. She sat in his dorm lounge for twelve hours, trying to act casual as if her slumped on a chair was the most normal thing in the world. She wanted to see if he was cheating on her when he said he was busy with schoolwork. After a few hours, she called her girlfriends and asked them to deliver her

food on shifts. She refused to leave her stakeout post. He did show up, alone, but of course, her casual shtick bombed. When he arrived, she was a wild-eyed feral female who'd lived on McNuggets for half a day. He never let her forget her stint as private dick.

3. *You Can't Treat the Right Man Wrong.* If it's not a law of nature, it should be. You can't treat the right man wrong. Conversely, you can't treat the wrong man right. In other words, "If he's really the one, you won't have to compromise yourself or values, or worry about every word you say." You cannot make someone love you. Stalking them and hoping they panic and give in doesn't work. Remember, we are all responsible for what we do, unless we are celebrities.

4. *Get It Straight From the (Gay) Horse's Mouth.* As thirty-six-year-old Suzanne says, "My gay guy friends help me not take male behavior too seriously. I am much more trusting of a man's opinion of another man. I sometimes second-guess advice from other girls who are in the same boat as me. It's almost like 'If a guy says it about another guy, it must be true.' "

5. *Don't Freak Out. That's Why You Have a Herd.* Think of your herd as your emotional insurance policy. A herd serves many purposes, including providing you diversity and options. But a real benefit is that you don't place all hopes on one man. Even if there's a man you want badly, having a herd takes the pressure off. Without excess pressure, you and the guys have a

chance to be yourselves. That's the ideal way to find out if you have enough shared feelings, interests, and values to form a stronger relationship.

6. *Be the Girlfriend, Don't Play One on TV.* Sometimes when I hear women talking about snagging a guy, they remind me of that commercial where the woman says, "I am not a doctor, but I play one on TV." Some women are more interested in looking like the girlfriend than actually being the girlfriend. Most guys don't want the superficial, high-maintenance woman. Thirty-two-year-old New York native Maria thought she was doing the right thing by focusing on hair, makeup, and clothes, but totally missed what her boyfriend really wanted. He wanted real bonding. She was only interested in playing a part, and in this case, her acting didn't win her any awards.

7. *Friends Don't Let Friends Drink and Dial.* There's a mythology surrounding girls and the drunken (and usually regretted afterwards) phone calls they make to guys. Remember the *Friends* episode in which a drunken Rachel calls Ross from a restaurant and leaves a message telling him, "I am over you. I am over you and that, my friend, is what they call closure"? She hangs up and tosses the phone into an ice bucket. But that kind of closure doesn't work. Had I known my friend Cathleen would drink and dial a former flame who ended their affair abruptly, I would have knocked the Merlot out of her hand. As she says, "In my younger, foolish days, I tracked down a guy I'd dated

and left him a voicemail telling him to 'Have a good life.' It was bad enough that our last date was a year prior to that call. To make it worse, one year later, I called him again after drinking too much. Ugh, live and learn. Recently I attended a conference where I could see women drinking too much, followed by calls to their boyfriends and husbands. I said, "Take my advice ladies, don't drink and dial."

8. *Don't Overestimate His Intentions.* I hate to see women waste time on the endless debate about men's intentions. It's almost like that joke:

Why did the chicken cross the road? *To get to the other side.*
Why did the man cross the road? *Who the hell knows? Why do they do anything?*

Cut your postdate worry in half by remembering this fact: women overestimate the evil of men's motives. You think men are acting awful when in fact they are just clueless and apathetic. Women blame themselves, take it personally, and then want to get back. That's a lot of time invested in someone who probably doesn't deserve it, ladies!

GETTING OVER A BREAKUP IS HARD TO DO

You're great, he's headed to ugly-old-man-land, and she's nothing but a gold-digging witch!

Ah, the many splendored reasons for breakups! As Paul Simon said, there are fifty ways to leave your lover. I think I've heard more than that from my women friends.

He cheated on you with the tart from his office. You cheated on him when he ignored you. He's an emotional two-year-old. He drinks (substitute "smokes, eats, or gambles") too much. He doesn't understand and support your spiritual path. He's got A.D.D. He just disappeared and you have no clue why (other than a hunch that straight men can be idiots). He hates your cats. He puts mayonnaise on liver and onions and calls it a meal.

Trust me, I have heard all the reasons for breaking up with him. I have been there at 2 a.m. listening to you alternate between a sob and a rant when he dumps you. When you dump him, I hear you alternate between a sob, a rant, and pity for the poor sucker. I am not sure which is worse. Either way, I now long for morning breakups so that I can spend my afternoons listening and trying to help, but still get uninterrupted nighttime sleep on the fateful breakup day. But it's the least I can do. After all, when my two-year relationship went south very suddenly, my poor friend Bonnie was on call. I still don't know if I've thanked her enough.

But the point is that I never want you to be Tammy Wynette, the little woman in the country song standing beside the man who done her wrong. Usually you have ample reasons to dump the dumb bastard. Women seem inherently fairer and more thoughtful than men in their decisions to end a relationship. And if he's dumped you, I say "good riddance." In most of the instances I can think of, it was a blessing in disguise. By the time I give you the "You're So Great-He's Headed to Ugly-Old-Man-Land-and-She's-Nothing-but-a-Gold-Digging-Witch-Who'll-Wreck-His-World-and-Leave-Him-Broke" speech, I am so sick of hearing about his errant ways that I want to break up with him myself.

To paraphrase the song "Fifty Ways to Leave Your Lover" for women: "Make a new plan, Ann. No need to be coy, Joy. Drop off the key, Lee. And get yourself free."

"Why do I rely on you so much?" my thirty-eight-year-old writer friend, Cathy, wondered. We were having coffee and I asked her why having a gay boyfriend was so important to her. "You are like this strange combination of friend, counselor, and muse, always uplifting me, especially during my rotten times. When I've had a breakup, just hearing, 'You're beautiful and smart and he wasn't good enough for you,' felt more sincere than hearing it from my girlfriends, who often have their own agendas and might have seen me, now newly single, as another threat. Gay men explain male behavior to me in a way that makes sense to me. But, being a gay man means you can also switch gears and give me the sweet, nurturing, 'fabulous woman' speech that I need to hear. There's something about getting a hug, a compliment, and a good talk from a man who obviously has no ulterior motives that does the trick for me."

It's your unalienable right as a woman with a gay boyfriend to expect that I'll get out the martini shaker when you're sad, and together we'll plot a fitting revenge against the scum-sucking bastard who made you sad. No matter what happens, I have at least 101 gay dating horror stories to remind you how much worse it could be.

Every type of breakup deserves its own supportive speech from your gay best friend. Who better than another man to convincingly tell you that all men are pigs? Who better than a gay man to frame that message in the sensitive, nurturing, and probably uncharitable language that will make you stop crying and actually listen? That's why I'm offering you speeches written just for you to cope with trying times:

HE CHEATED ON YOU WITH THE TART FROM HIS OFFICE.

So he ran off with the tart from his office? Given how out of shape he is, what's really surprising to me is that he can actually run. Don't worry. Karma is a boomerang. Just sit back and count the weeks until reality gives him the slap in the face you didn't have the chance to deliver. Once the thrill of being sneaky is gone and he realizes he has to face her every day, he'll see that he's a helluva lot more trapped than he was with you. These office romances that start on the sly are always time bombs just waiting to go off. You don't even have to wish him ill, because once it detonates, he's going to have no one to blame but himself. Just remember, they'll have to live with the knowledge that both of them are cheaters. How deep do you think the "river of trust" will run in that relationship? Can you say, "Shallow as a dry lake bed?"

HE'S AN EMOTIONAL TWO-YEAR-OLD AND DOESN'T DESERVE A REAL WOMAN.

The prerequisite for dating a guy like that is a master's degree in child psychology. But it's not your fault that his emotional development ended at age two. Faced with this childish idiot, even the renowned psychologist Piaget would have thrown up his hands and said "next." Piaget said children cannot undertake certain tasks until they are psychologically mature enough to do so. So why anyone ever let this guy out of the crib to date a real woman like you is beyond me. Listen, if Piaget were here, he'd say count your blessings that you are not changing this man's emotional diaper for the next thirty years. He takes the concept of infantile egocentrism, the belief that you are the center of the universe and everything revolves around you, to a new level. I say that, after age twenty-five, if a man hasn't learned how to share and treat his partner, he just grows horns and becomes a selfish and all-too-commonplace "aging manboy."

HE DRINKS TOO MUCH AND COUNT YOUR BLESSINGS HE LEFT, BECAUSE IT AIN'T GONNA BE PRETTY IN TEN YEARS.

The Alcoholics Anonymous definition of "insanity" is "doing the same thing repeatedly and expecting a different outcome every time." It's right on target. Addiction to booze (substitute any substance or damaging behavior here) is a progressive problem. You didn't cause him to have it, and you cannot cure it on your own. Make your case for him to get help. But if you find yourself preaching this until you are a harpy, then it's time to move on. Don't pretend that it will all be fine one bright morning. If he does nothing, nothing will change and it ain't gonna be pretty in a few years. Are you lulled into a false sense of security just because you have a man in the house? Just remember that you have a better chance of raising the Titanic than of rousing him should someone break into your house. There was nothing in that house he really cared about much, starting with himself, so the stakes weren't very high anyway. You could be the one thing that keeps him from getting help. Once you realize that you can't help him, you are free. So take care of yourself. Too bad you didn't have a man who could challenge you to grow, change, and live in a healthy way. But next to the alcohol, you didn't stand a chance to share those positive things with him.

HE LEAVES YOU AND YOU HAVE NO IDEA WHY.

When you were together, he always said he'd die for you. Now that he left for no good reason, at least no reason he chose to share with you, I think it's time he kept his promise. I want you to take pen to paper and write him the following farewell: "In the weeks since you left, I'm so miserable without you. It's almost like you're here. Looking back over the time we had together, I can't help but wonder: What the fuck was I thinking? If I could go back in time, I'd 'unshave' my legs before each and every 'date' that ended up with me watching you watch television. When I think of the wasted razors, I could cry. It's true that you had your good points. You had an even disposition (miserable all the time). You gave me so much (like a need for therapy). I learned to appreciate the little things in life (my real friends, vibrator, Netflix, Chinese food delivery, and, of course, your penis). And I must admit, you brought religion into my life (I never believed in hell until I met you, that's for sure). To borrow from the Dolly Parton song, I want you to know that, no matter what happened between us, I will always love . . . the false image I had of you." Then stick the letter in your drawer and let's call that closure.

HE DOESN'T UNDERSTAND AND SUPPORT YOUR SPIRITUAL PATH.

It's one thing to have different beliefs. It's another if he doesn't support you on yours. And this can come in many forms. Inability to let you talk about things that are important to you is one form. Disparaging remarks couched in humor is another, as well as my personal favorite. Humor is the great defense of passive aggressives everywhere. The "But-I-I-I-I-Was-Just-Joking" defense has been used by passive aggressives to mask their true intentions since the days of Judas Iscariot. So get centered. Find your inner Buddha. Listen closely for the small, still voice within. And where you hear it scream out, "Run! He's Not The One!" then listen to it and feel good about letting go. With love and a good pair of Nikes, of course.

THINK ABOUT THE MOST BORING NIGHT YOU EVER HAD WITH HIM. IMAGINE THAT FOR THE NEXT THIRTY YEARS.

Remember that night when he just couldn't be bothered to move from the sofa? Remember that it wasn't a night, but actually a period of two months? Maybe you don't remember because you are trying to give him the benefit of the doubt, so it's no surprise that your memory timeline is distorted. That's OK because mine isn't. I remember all the conversations we've had about this. You keep making excuses for why he's not more excited to be with you. If a helicopter dropped him in the middle of a football field, with the remote control at one end, and you at the other, which do you think he'd run to? Exactly. So when you tell me he's not enough for you, listen to what you are saying. You have a right to be with someone who sees you as someone to cherish, not as a convenience, right up there with other conveniences like pizza delivery and digital cable.

HE WAS A CREEP, BUT WHAT AM I GOING TO DO WITHOUT A MAN AROUND?

You'll live more peacefully, that's what. For those times when you miss the false sense of safety that having a physical presence in your house might have provided: Yes, there was occasionally a warm body in the next room. There was a warm body that represented unhealthy stagnation. A warm body that didn't seem to appreciate your hot body. It's good to have illusions taken away. They weren't real. The only safety in life is to feel safe. To the man who walked out, say goodbye, ask for insights into the lessons learned so you can move on and not stay stuck where you were, and look forward to new beginnings. In the end, we're all on our personal road anyway. We share the road with others but we're on it alone. Your job in life is to make your road one of health, love, growth, and as much happiness for yourself and others as possible.

Bobbi, formerly married to a creep, told me that the best relationship advice she's ever gotten was from a gay friend after her marriage ended badly and her husband left. Her pal Jerry told her to "Change the locks on the door. Just change the locks. From that moment on I became able to control my life at a devastating time. He said, 'This is your place; you control what goes in this place. He can't just come and go.' It gave me back control of my life. It's one of the reasons why I kept control of my house that I still live in now. Jerry was a businessman, and his practical point of view helped me see things clearly. He definitely took on the role of protector. He thought Ted acted morally wrong to me. It harkens back to the gay culture existing in this small space that it occupies in the larger culture; the people in it need to be able to protect themselves from the harshness that's flung at them constantly. So that protective veil extends to others outside the gay community, to anyone the gay guys care about."

Here's what I want you to do when you've either just ended a relationship or are seriously contemplating doing so. Follow these tips from a protective guy who hates to see you lose valuable time by worrying about a loser who, in the long run, will end up being a blip on the fabulous screen of your life.

1. *Avoid Salmon Days.* Have salmon for lunch, preferably grilled with a little dill sauce on the side. But I don't want you to have "salmon days." You know what salmon days are. They are the days when you spend all your time swimming upstream, fighting the tide, only to get screwed and die in the end.

2. *Listen to Maya!* My friend Shane was fortunate enough to take a college writing class from the fabulous Maya Angelou. In addition to writing advice, she imparted the following bit of wisdom that he and I have adopted as our dating motto. She said, "When a man tells you who he is through his actions, believe them." Thank you, Maya.

3. *It Is Better to Have Loved and Lost. It's True.* Alfred Lord Tennyson claimed, " 'Tis better to have loved and lost than never to have loved at all." Big Al said it, but he never met Bobbi's husband. Joking aside, it is better to have loved and lost. Love makes you realize you are fully alive. It's our deepest connection with another person. The good memories are always yours. Even the so-called "bad" experiences make you the

person you are, and become good if you learn from them and move on. So I would add that it's better to have loved and lost, as long as you learned and made peace with it.

4. *Alert! New Disease Strikes Women Across America. It's Called "Bastard Affective Disorder."* Judging by the straight women I know who've contracted this relatively new syndrome, I'd say that awareness of it is gaining credibility and momentum. It becomes chronic after a series of bad dates. Some of the symptoms include watching the TV show *Cops* to see bad men get tackled and handcuffed. In the most severe cases, straight women have retreated to celibate communes for up to five years. After bad dates, you might have the urge to remove yourself from dating, eat junk food (ice cream tops the list), and replace men with objects that require double A batteries. Don't. The bastards aren't worth it.

5. *Maybe He's Not That Into You.* And so what if he's not? As a gay man who's wasted too much time analyzing why certain guys weren't into me, I can finally say that it's very liberating to realize that, no matter who you are and what you look like, you're not going to be everyone's type. It's hard for gay men and cool straight girls to accept this. We both bolt out of the gate racing to be liked. Remember what the character Berger told the *Sex and the City* ladies when Miranda wondered why a man didn't pursue a deeper relationship with her? "Maybe he's just not that into you,"

Berger said simply. Maybe he's not. No matter how cute you are, you aren't going to be everyone's cup of tea. Straight men understand this better because they're raised to be proactive and to choose, rather than wait to be chosen.

6. *Access Your Inner Katharine Hepburn and Move On!* Accessing your inner Katharine Hepburn means listening to the crusty New England Yankee within who tells you to just get on with it, regardless if "it" is a man, a bad break at work, or difficulty with your family. There's always something you can do to move a little bit forward. Work out, redo your home, add a few new friends to your circle, break your routine, or do something that's "totally not you." In other words, rebuild your life. If your positive actions are fueled by the fires of retaliation (I'll show him!), then great! At least it's a productive way to deal with your feelings. Living well really is the best revenge, and I will add, living well on your own terms. How's this for motivation? Staying miserable because of a bad former relationship just might mean that guy was right about you.

7. *It Could Be Worse.* No matter how bad your last dating experience or relationship was, it could have been worse. There's a Buddhist phrase that roughly translates to, "When you can't be thankful for what you have or what happened, be thankful for what you were spared." The gay boyfriend version of this Buddhist entreaty is, "When you can't be thankful that the lummox left you high and dry, just wait a year and see

what's happening in his life. Chances are you'll get a taste of sweet karmic justice." So many women I know, who thought their lives were ending because a relationship with a man ceased, saw him in a different light a year or so later after the magic wore off. They saw him repeating the same stupid patterns, unhappy, and generally not getting it. Your mistake was in thinking it was because of you. Rarely is bad behavior really provoked in a "one off" kind of way. It's usually a character trait that follows a person like a monkey on his back until he finally deals with it.

11

SO YOU'RE THIRTY-NINE, WANT MARRIAGE AND BABIES, AND HAVE NO IMMEDIATE PROSPECTS?

Let's start working on the alternatives; they might be better than you think.

Women who think the only way to be happy is to be married with children should meet thirty-four-year-old Tina. She has three kids under the age of ten, a husband who's increasingly married to his work, and is living in a suburb that's so far north of downtown Atlanta that it should be called a sub suburb.

She worked in public relations until her husband, Matt, swept her off her feet. When she finally landed about a year and a half later, her life was radically different from the one she'd initially chosen. She didn't get to see her friends as much. She hated the fact that I was available only for phone consultations (never an adequate substitute for a long lunch). The truth about kids is that as much as she loved them, they were a ton of work, all mouths and heinies and screaming demands. In retrospect, she thinks she followed a little girl's fairy tale dream by getting married too young at age twenty-six. The problem with fairy tales is that they aren't always fully thought out. What happened to Cinderella a few years after moving into the castle with Prince Charming? Did it get a little stuffy in there? Did she get cabin fever? Did sweeping out the fireplace start to look pretty good to her because at least she'd get some quiet time alone?

Tina is not an "anti–traditional marriage and kids" poster child. But for single women out there who've questioned straying from traditional paths of marriage and kids, Tina's story is important. It's a reminder that the grass is always greener on the other side. It reaffirms that there are pros and cons to all of our choices. Sometimes the reason women follow traditional paths has more to do with fairy tales than real life. I am under no such illusions. I didn't grow up with fairy tales of what was supposed to happen to me. It didn't cross my mind that I could get married or have a family. The prospects for a gay man were incredibly limited, and most of the stereotypes such as Bitter Old Queen and Aging Peter Pan weren't very appealing. Of course, the rules for gays are changing now. But these mindset changes are happening pretty late in the game for a lot of us. Only now are some of us opening our minds to possibilities of marriage and kids. You know what? I am glad I didn't have to contend with the powerful forces of traditional fairy tales as I made and continue to make choices about how to live. It's made me think more like a pioneer.

On the other side of the fence from Tina is Sandy, a thirty-eight-year-old successful consultant. She wants to get married and have babies, but there's no guy in sight. Gay men certainly have major issues around aging, but the drastic, final biological clock is a uniquely female experience. I've only known three straight women who knew unequivocally that they never wanted marriage or kids. They thumbed their nose at the biological clock.

All the others have gone through periods of questioning that ranged from mild to severe. Sandy is at the severe end of the continuum. She's convinced herself that her sole reason for being is to marry the right man and have at least two children.

It's been helpful to her to point out these alternatives:

- Adoption.

- Having a child without getting married, through natural or alternative methods such as in vitro fertilization.

- Recognizing the value of being an aunt, confidante, or friend to a younger person.

- Focusing on a fabulous partner, but without having kids.

- Volunteering with kids if she loves kids so much.

- Seeing the world.

My role isn't just talking about the relative benefits of each of these options. My role is showing them in real life. On a daily basis, I am living outside the traditional norms. That's one of the reasons my advice on this topic has resonance. Even for partnered gay men, who consider food shopping in the 'burbs the most exciting thing they'll do all week, we're still white elephants when it comes to traditional societal expectations. Of course, there's a cost to being different, but there's freedom attached to it as well. I want you to feel that same freedom. The life you didn't imagine might be better than the one you did.

"My gay friends want me to make good choices, and they offer me options, but without pushing me to do a specific thing," says Melissa. "They want to really advise me, the others are trying to maneuver me."

Gay friends might influence your thoughts about alternatives to traditional paths of marriage and children because they are out in the world now in a way that's never been possible before. We are inventive—inventing our lives and the groups we travel in—out of necessity.

As Bobbi, a fifty-year-old entrepreneur, says, "I have a sense of appreciation of the inventiveness of how gay people are making it work for themselves. Here's our situation, how can we make it the best? There are a lot of women like me who are in our fifties, single now and thinking in different terms of how to work out the latter part of our lives in a whole new way. It doesn't matter if we are never married, divorced, or widowed. Even women who have kids, with all the geographical separation, are finding it necessary to form different types of community and family. Especially if you put in place living wills and trusts, you can make a workable community for yourself. I haven't made a child but I've made a community."

Bobbi adds, "Because gay men are making the shit up as you go along, there's no template for you to follow about how a gay man lives in the world today openly. Of course you understand what I am facing."

When I consider finding meaning in a nontraditional life, I think of this quote from George Bernard Shaw: "This is the true joy in life, the being used for a purpose recognized by yourself as a mighty one; the being thoroughly worn out before you are thrown on the scrap heap; the being a force of nature instead of a feverish selfish little clod of ailments and grievances complaining that the world will not devote itself to making you happy."

That quote reminds me that all of us create meaning; we don't find it. Sometimes the life you end up with can be better than the one you planned. I know of several women who are happier post what's now referred to as "starter marriages," the short-lived first marriage that ends in divorce with no kids, no property, and no regrets. For example, thirty-five-year-old Mary grew up in Long Island with fantasies of the perfect prince who'd ensure her "happily ever after." She wanted to get married so badly that one of her friends told me, "I am convinced that she willed the successful lawyer she married into her life." After the wedding came a baby, and Mary was looking to make a little extra money from home. She'd given up her day job as a human resource director only to discover a passion for creating fashion accessories. She found a passion in life that sadly she lacked in her marriage. Soon, driven by talent and her love for her work, Mary's "little home business hobby" soared. But then it was almost like her fairy tale spell was broken. It turns out she didn't need the prince to take care of her after all. She'd made it on her own. As painful as it is for her to realize, all she wanted was the fairy tale, she didn't really love the guy. In her words, "He wasn't enough for me."

Women like Mary thought that marriage was life's next step. They hit a milestone, look around and say, "What's next?" That's a terrible reason to get married or have a baby. When I asked Mary if she had any regrets, she said she "regrets the marriage but not the baby. Women may regret marriage but never the babies."

Sometimes you'll be faced with a choice of being single or settling for the "He's just not enough for me" guy. Just remember that after the Cinderella fairy tale comes the reality. Make sure all the elements of a happy reality are in place when you find your fairy tale. The thing that irritates me most about fairy tales is that they are usually about a woman being chosen, rather than choosing.

Maybe you want the traditional life or maybe you want the raucous life. As Bobbi says, "I am the standard bearer of making the most of being single, going to Bruce Springsteen shows, and living a traveling lifestyle. My house is where my married girlfriends all come when they want to have a break. I miss not having had a kid. But I don't miss the marriage part. I don't care at all about marriage. I do whatever I can to keep kids in my life. I am a friend to my friends' kids—I try to have personal relationships with them. My friend has two boys, ages nine and six. On Friday I come home from work and take them to the park. I rent the movies they watch and listen to the music they listen to, so I am a repository for them. They have one cool adult place to go that's not their parents' house. I didn't have adults like this when I was a kid."

It is fascinating to see that women are sometimes the

harshest critics of women's choices. I remember overhearing a colleague say of another high-powered colleague who opted to leave her high paying publishing job to focus on motherhood, "Women worked so hard to get where we are for that?" I don't want you to waste your time worrying about what other people think, either. To quote Maya Angelou again, "What other people think of you is none of your business." When we fight for our rights, it's a fight for choices. That doesn't mean you have to nix marriage and motherhood. Nor should you feel guilty about focusing on alternative paths. If I did what people expected of me, I'd either be closeted and married or immersed in "gay ghetto mentality" such as dressing, thinking, and looking like a gay archetype.

Here are some points to ponder next time you find yourself contemplating a nontraditional path:

1. *Think Twice About Your Options.* You are allowed to create your own life, with goals that are yours alone, not remnants from your mother, father, or society. If knowing that gay men are blazing a trail through leftover expectations laid on us as we cut fabulous swaths to our authentic lives, then great! Maybe the pioneering is worth it. Thirty-nine-year-old Atlanta native Donna says, "Seeing my gay friends makes me braver about being unmarried and not having kids. I watch them explore their lives and find out what it is they want out of life. Marriage is great and I want it, but your options have made me think twice about my own. I feel like I am inventing my life."

2. *There Are Many Ways to Have Kids in Your Life.* I love being an uncle. In a way, I am fortunate that I didn't have the strong urge to have children. Being an aunt, uncle, godfather, godmother, or friend to kids is enriching enough. You don't need ownership to feel the connection or make a difference in a child's life.

3. *Living the "Samantha" Lifestyle Has Its Advantages.* Face it. Fun is important. It sounds silly, but it's true. I see so many couples, straight and gay, struggling in their unhappy relationships. Living the "Samantha" lifestyle has its advantages. The blond-haired, forty-something vixen from *Sex and the City* showed women that you could be in charge of your own life, unapologetically sexual, and happily connected with work and friends. Women are saddled with way too much relationship baggage. There's the "Aren't you married yet?" steamer trunk, the "Your life doesn't start until you have a man" suitcase, and the myopic "This is what society expects" carry-on. Travel lighter, let go of some of the bags, and then go after what's really important to you.

4. *Life (and Its Options) Come in Stages.* One secret of a happy life is to accept each stage as we glide through. There's the crazy twenties when we figure out who we are. During the thirties, most of us gain some direction, and options abound. By the time we reach forty, some options aren't as likely. You have to allow your goals to be self-adjusting. What you accepted as the norm at one stage may not be the norm at another. As Cathleen

says, "In the current dating situation I am in, if I didn't know you were in a nontraditional relationship, I would have given up on the long-distance relationship I am in with a recently divorced guy. I am forty-four, and I still want the traditional paths. Sometimes I look around at other women my age and see them living their lives as if they are still twenty-one years old, with a future of traditional options ahead of them."

5. *Forget the Fairy Tale.* The reason fairy tales are such powerful mythology for women in our society is that no one ever tells you what happens next! That's a problem. Does Cinderella like living in the castle after she married the prince, or does she feel trapped? Does Snow White like being rescued, or does she miss communal living with her friends the dwarfs? For all we know, the old lady who lived in the shoe, with so many kids that she didn't know what to do, started out as a young bride with big dreams that got waylaid by too many damn diapers. The point is that weddings are to marriage what fairy tales are to life. They are the party, the draw, and the excitement that leads us down paths of lives that twist and turn. It's better to walk those paths with clear vision and make your choices accordingly.

6. *Timing Is Everything.* Mr. Right isn't really Mr. Right unless he comes at the right time. Keep this in mind as you fight the pressures of societal pressures and the biological clock. The early bird may get the worm, but the second mouse gets the cheese. As thirty-three-year-

old Melanie from Seattle says, "I want marriage and kids but I do not want the wrong guy at the wrong time. I have seen too many of my thirtysomething girl-friends panic, race to the altar for their starter marriage, and then get stuck in a life that doesn't work for them at all." Melanie says she, "Gets pangs for kids. That's normal after thirty." But her friend Richard found a way to minimize the pangs. "When the clock goes off and I'm craving the pitter patter of little feet, he puts shoes on my cat."

7. *Avoid the Guilt Trip Trap.* I am aware every day that someone, somewhere thinks I should either abstain like a monk or ship off to Hetero Conversion Therapy camp. The same people think you should curb that silly career, get married, and give birth to four children ASAP. If that's not your idea of bliss, ignore them. I certainly plan on ignoring them as much as humanly possible. I wouldn't look good in a drab monk's robe, baking carb-laden bread, and I never liked camp. Let's make a deal to avoid the guilt trip trap. "Thank God for my gay friends and like-minded female friends. I feel better about not wanting to have kids," says Sarah, a thirty-five-year-old businesswoman in Virginia. "I am so tired of the whole woman guilt trip, that we're self-ish if we don't want kids. The worst part is that it's per-petuated by other women."

8. *What's Most Important Are the True Connections.* Wed-dings are beautiful, parties can be a blast, but love is what really counts. Weddings are a day, love is a life-

time, or at least it's the bulk of time you spend together. As Cathleen says, "I've learned from gay friends in committed relationships who'd get married if they could. Seeing their relationships makes me see that it's not necessary to formalize love. There are other ways to find a committed relationship than wearing a white dress and having a big party." In this society your option to be a blushing bride in white, walking down the fairy tale aisle, comes with an expiration date. What does that have to do with the depth of your feelings for your guy? What is that compared to finding a person you care about, who cares about you, and committing your lives to each other? Not much.

12

THE TEN THINGS ONLY YOUR GAY BEST FRIEND NEEDS TO KNOW

When to ask but not tell all with a
boyfriend—and where never to go with him.

By now I hope you know the basics of boyfriend communication:

- If he asks you how many men you've slept with—no matter how cool he seems to be about the subject of you and your sex life BH (before him)—always make sure he answers first. Then answer him with a figure that's half the one he quotes.

- If you are PMS-ing, please, for God's sake, tell him at the onset. Don't wait and tell him two days later when he finds you crying and agitated, or after you've ripped him a new one, as they say on the loading docks.

- Worst of all, if he's offended you and you're pissed at him, don't respond with "Nothing" when the honestly confused poor sot asks you what's wrong.

But those are just the basics. I know there are things on your mind, feelings you want to express, secrets you want to share, and forbidden thoughts you want to confide. *Tell me, not him.* I can take it. I am your gay boyfriend and I am unfazed by your deepest secrets. After all the dark and dank gay male secrets I have heard, nothing you say at this point will make me recoil in disgust or judge you.

Your man might not recoil either, but does he need to know that you learned sex secrets from you gay male friend? No. "My first gay male best friend John gave me advice on how to give a blow job," says Cathleen. "We went on a road trip to visit a friend from high school. Along the way, I got step-by-step instructions that were honestly the best clinical advice I've gotten on the subject. Girls are judgmental, shy, and don't have the expertise. There was less shame in talking to John about it. And he knew more."

Does he need a translator sometimes? Yes. *Est-il un âne parfois? Oui!* Everyone knows that straight men and women don't speak the same language. It's exciting to be in a foreign country with men who speak a different language. *Apportez sur les hommes beaux!* But it's much better with a translator. Fear not, *mon petit.* Gay boyfriends are the bridge between two languages. We'll act as interpreter.

Does he need to know all about your past? No. But sometimes you just want to talk about an ex, like the one who lit a bonfire on the beach and held you all night, both of you wrapped in a blanket looking at the stars? The moon glow wore off and he turned out to be a total jerk, but oh, what a night! Sometimes you need to revisit it ever so briefly, though you wouldn't trade the fabulous relationship you have for the world. Or maybe you just want to immerse in your feelings about an issue, with no interest in solving or fixing anything.

As Carol says, "My friend David doesn't just know about my past, he's lived it with me. My husband is the greatest guy in the world, but he's just not as comfortable talking about the 'feelings' stuff. This is why the combination of my husband and my gay best friend are the perfect man. All of my needs are taken care of; heart, soul and body."

As convenient as it would be to have all your needs met by one person, it's not very realistic. Ever since I stopped expecting that, my relationships have improved tenfold. Too often we store up everything we need to express in this world until we are as tightly coiled as cobras. Then our mate comes home from a long day of work. Bursting with neediness, we strike. Sometimes the relationship problem isn't that your needs are getting met, it's that you have too many needs. Spread the need around. Diversify your needs portfolio. Make your relationship more like a friendship and your friendships more romantic. Before you get any wild ideas, what that means is expand and deepen your circle of friends. You'll be less needy and more able to appreciate your mate's good points.

And if you face any jealousy from your man about your close gay male friends, remind him that he could accompany you to the Madonna concert, listen to a two-hour exploration of your family dynamics, or revisit *Sex and the City* for an all-day DVD marathon. I bet the jealousy will then disappear faster than you can say "Sports bar."

Can you really blame him for heading to the sports bar? I

can't. I completely empathize with the guy. We all need our inner sanctums of retreat.

At the end of the day, it's up to every woman to figure out what's better left *unsaid* or *undone* in her relationship. There's always gray area when you're timing a key revelation or broaching a touchy subject. But the women in my life are a living testimony to the ten top things you should never, ever ask your man to do with you. Consider laminating this list and keeping it with you at all times.

The Ten Things You Should Never, Ever, Ever Ask Your Man to Do with You (But It's Okay if It's Your Gay Best Friend)

1. *Comparison Shop for Clothes or Makeup, or Contribute More Than a Cursory Comment on Your Wardrobe Choice.* "Do not talk about awesome new moisturizers. Even some gay friends don't want to hear about it, but for my boyfriend, it's like fingernails on a blackboard if I start comparing Estēe Lauder to Clarins," says Jill, thirty-three-year-old retail manager in Texas.

2. *Have a Long Lunch with Your Female Pals.* You may substitute "lunch" with "all-day marathon of *Sex and the City* DVDs." Either way, estrogen overdose for him. Most straight men would implode. If I had to spend an entire day watching Jean Claude Van Damme movies (especially without an interpreter to break through that thick accent and tell me what the hell he's saying between kickboxes), I'd be ready to act in *Fight Club: The Sequel.*

3. *Plan the Menu of a Party, Especially if You're Trying to Impress Anyone with Your Taste.* Can you think of anything more futile than asking a typical straight guy to help you plan a party? I can't. He's like Rodney King meets Costco. (Can't we all just get along with high quantities of salty snacks, burgers, and finger food?!) He's not interested in your severe contemplation of how guests will mix and mingle, new and cutting-edge hors d'oeuvres, or the perfect music mix.

4. *Hang Out in the Bathroom with You While You Do Any of the Following:* facial mud mask, routine feminine hygiene procedures, eyebrow shaping, home leg-wax. Would you want him there anyway? I think something is terribly wrong if the answer is yes. Honey, you need to cultivate mystery in a relationship, so let's start with the bathroom, okay? Besides, who better than an urban gay man to understand the demands and pressures of having to look fantastic? If there's a way to firm it, smooth it, or buff it, we'll know.

5. *Watch Chick Flicks Like* Beaches *with You.* I once saw a straight man on Superbowl Sunday crying at a matinee of the film *Beaches*. He was dressed in typical straight guy garb: flannel open shirt, jeans, and hiking boots. But this was a broken man. Trust me, he wasn't crying because of Bette, the sadness of the story, or even Barbara Hershey's inflated lips (those made me cry, I admit). He was a sad sack. I sat there with two gay friends, all of us wondering what this poor straight man had done to deserve such cruel and inhuman punishment. I wanted to

go up to him, do the straight guy hug thing (hand to back, pulling away immediately, no frontal touching at all, anywhere) and slip him twenty dollars so he could cab home ASAP to his beloved sports programs.

6. *Overanalyze Your Female Coworker's Hidden Agenda.* It's not like all straight men give bad advice. They don't. It's just short. I mean s-h-o-r-t. When straight guys are done dispensing advice, they're done. Even when they have good perspectives on an issue, they make their point once and then they aren't interested in talking about it anymore. Unless you want to hear, "Avoid her. She's trouble. Case closed," midway through the complicated love-hate relationship you have with your "work cubicle neighbor," save it for me. I may end up telling you the same thing, but I'll say it at least five different ways, with empathy.

7. *Go to a Wedding Shower or Baby Shower.* (This applies doubly if you're ovulating.) I read recently that more men are attending wedding and baby showers than ever before. That might be true. I didn't read that they like them. To me, taking a straight man to a wedding shower or baby shower is just fraught with potential disaster. You know he doesn't want to "ooh and ahh" over the gifts. He's not filled with patience over how emotionally loaded these events are for you, either. Why should he be? From his perspective, you are dragging him to this. You should be *grateful.* Of course, from your perspective, he needs to be your man-in-waiting, ready with a Kleenex or at least an attentive ear.

8. *Make a Night of It at the Gay Bars, Just for the Hell of It.* Of course you love hanging out at gay bars occasionally, at least the upscale ones. Why wouldn't you? You get to play with a preponderance of good-looking men without the pressure or sexual tension. He, on the other hand, has three options: total boredom, managing unwanted interest, or, hopefully, finding some fun gay guys who'll make him feel welcome.

9. *Spend More Than a Week with Your Mother, if Her Presence Brings Out Your Latent Bratty Side.* If your mother is in any way overbearing, consider giving him a break when she visits. I can handle her. I "do" moms exceptionally well.

10. *Go to a Boy Band* Concert* (*Substitute "American Idol Tour," "Ricky Martin," or "Barry Manilow"). My friend Paul, straight as an arrow, found himself in a straight man's no-win situation. His wife Lisa secured free tickets close to the stage for the American Idol concert. This was her version of front row at the Lakers game. Enthusiasm for *that* he could definitely understand. Wearing a new outfit she bought to cover her thirty-year-old body, she'd let her mushy, *Teen Beat*–reading, inner eight-year-old out for the night. Midway through, a clearly fidgety Paul was granted an honorable discharge from the Idol concert. Lisa and I waved good-bye to him as thousands of twelve-year-old girls and five adults (including us) swooned over Kelly Clarkson singing "A Moment Like This."

The Ten Things You Should Never, Ever, Ever Say to Your Man (Tell Me Instead)

From time to time, you might be tempted to say any or all of the following to your man. When the temptation strikes, strike back and don't do it! Tell me instead.

1. I had a hot sex dream last night about my ex-boyfriend. He was a sturdy land baron. I was a lusty French maid. We made love for hours in his chateau in the Swiss Alps.

2. I stalked you early in our relationship when I was hopelessly insecure and untrusting. I followed you around one night, trailing you in my car for hours. You were incredibly boring. I was incredibly relieved.

3. I caught your dad checking me out as I bent over to pick up my keys. You know, the old man still has some fire left. I hope you are like that when you are his age.

4. Will you watch the new seasons of *The Bachelor* and *For Love or Money?* with me? Watching reality TV together makes me feel close with you. Don't ask me why.

5. Does this dress make my butt look too big? What should I wear then?

6. Your mother is a heinous, controlling witch, and you are her clueless little lapdog sometimes, aren't you?

7. I want to spend the day talking about the complexities of our relationship. Sometimes, I just feel so complicated, and you just seem so simple.

8. My girlfriend is out to sabotage me, but she's doing it in totally covert ways. Let's analyze the minutia of her Machiavellian behavior and figure out how to stop her.

9. Your best friend is a total moron. I don't care if you've known him since high school. I am sure he was a puerile moron then, too. The fact that you like him so much really makes me wonder about you.

10. I know that's your opinion about (insert subject here), but, deep down, how do you really *feel* about it?

The Fifteen Most Repeated Things You Tell Your Gay Boyfriend

Of course, you want to help your gay boyfriend, too. Trust me, we all need some gentle and not-so-gentle reminders occasionally. Gay men often need the advice of their sane girlfriends to get back on track. Based on my interviews with women, here are the fifteen most often repeated things they wish their gay boyfriends would learn from them.

1. Do not ditch your girlfriends when you go out to a club.

2. Work as hard on your insides as you do on your outsides. It wouldn't kill you to skip the clubs a little more so your life is more diverse and you don't get into a "gay ghetto" rut.

3. Stop worrying about aging so much. Get a reality check now. Save some fun for later. It is a typical man thing to go wild when you are young, but for gay men, it's twice as bad. Save some. Don't feel so panicked about doing it all before you are older, which, by the way, does not mean thirty.

4. Be nicer to each other. They say women are tough on each other, but gay men are sometimes each other's worst enemies with too much attitude and arrogance. You know that line in *Terminator*, "You humans, it is in your nature to destroy one another." Don't let Arnold be right about you gay guys.

5. Just because you came out later than some other gay men, you don't have to feel like you are in an eternal race to play catch up when it comes to dating and guys.

6. It's not a crime to be more commitment oriented and emotionally fulfilled.

7. Be safer sexually.

8. Don't be so closeted. Get over it. Don't you want people to know you?

9. It's good to celebrate your lives. Fight for your civil rights and marriage. But remember this: as long as you have love and commitment, it doesn't matter what form it takes, religious or civil. People in my generation are already suspicious of marriage since we grew up as kids of divorce.

10. When it comes to shopping, don't be such a brand whore.

11. You have the world by a string, if you will only pay attention to what's important and not get too distracted by what's not important. I want to prod you to realize your real dreams.

12. It's okay to admit you are little jealous when you see me with another guy.

13. Pay attention to kids. They are their own reward.

14. It's okay to have a favorite DJ, but for God's sake, they are not the new messiahs.

15. You've run amuck with "manscaping."

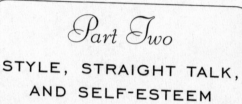

Part Two

STYLE, STRAIGHT TALK, AND SELF-ESTEEM

BARGAIN SHOPPING IS A GAME—PLAY TO WIN!

Ten tips for making affordably stylish
purchases, whether you shop
Versace or Target.

Sad, dead eyes staring ahead. Feet shuffling slowly step by step. Mental confusion with every pause. Sounds like the description of someone in *One Flew Over the Cuckoo's Nest*, doesn't it? The only thing that distinguishes your trip to any other huge department store from a stay in a mental home is the fact that you are pushing a shopping cart.

As only your gay best friend can, I want to guide you through the perilous waters of too many options, eager beaver sales clerks, and a variety of clothing materials that range from polyester freshly made in a test tube to world-class cotton and wool.

"Let's get real, honey, you can look a little cheap." That gorgeous nugget of wisdom comes from none other than style princess Paris Hilton, in an interview with *Elle*. I am hoping that she meant to say "casual," not "cheap." Cheap is a porn video that gets distributed on the Internet. Casual is a state of mind that is also reflected in your appearance. It doesn't mean cheap man-made fabrics or lack of quality. I share the dream every woman has when she walks into Target that she'll find shoes that look like Manolos, wear like sneakers, and cost like Payless.

We can all agree that it's no shame to find and rejoice in a bargain. In fact, it's a source of pride and often a crucial element in the success or failure of retail therapy. Engage your gaydar at any given Walmart, Target, or Bed, Bath and Beyond, and you'll see plenty of gay men checking out the sheet thread count, underwear sales, and designer kitchenware (often hidden next to the cheap stuff). While it's true that, as a group, gay men have an elevated aesthetic, we aren't afraid to hit the malls with a vengeance, armed with a discerning eye toward quality in those store aisles. Martha entered the Kmart arena, Richard Graves took his kitchenware designs to Target, and even Gucci has outlet stores. Now it's time to expound on secrets you have to know if you are going to shop with a gay man's voracity and eye for detail. Who better to point out the quality difference between the crappy poly/rayon blend that makes up a flawless disco shirt and a sheer crap blouse?

"The places that I shop, like Mood Indigo in New York's Soho neighborhood, are all managed by gay guys. Invariably I am drawn to furniture stores and shops owned or managed by a gay guy," says fifty-year-old Bobbi. "The gay guys just like cool stuff. They embrace the bold color, details, and the cultural aspects that I have fallen for hook, line, and sinker. When I was growing up, my mother made sure everything matched. As an adult, I have learned how to shake it up. Since coming into my own, I like unique things. Recently a few gay guys came to visit my eclectic house and said, 'You know how to shop.' I took that as the ultimate compliment. The typical suburban style, where everything matches and blends in, is something I don't want."

In some ways it's become harder and harder to express your individuality. The world sometimes seems like one giant shopping mall with the same places: Starbucks, Banana Republic, The Gap, J. Crew, Ann Taylor, and other brands dominate. With television and media in our faces 24/7, we're all inundated with the same images constantly. It becomes that much more important to express your individuality.

"It's the creativity," says twenty-nine-year-old Paula. "My gay friends help me see that it's not about expensive versus inexpensive at all. It's about creatively approaching what you buy in order to physically manifest your personal style. They are experts at the fabulous mix and match. We're in such a 'designer label combined with celebrity' culture, from J.Lo and P. Diddy to Calvin Klein and Donatella Versace. You have to work harder to stand out."

That means you have to get competitive. The majority of gay guys don't watch sports on their plasma high-definition televisions, but don't think for a minute we aren't as competitive as straight men about everything. We are. We're men. We're competitive about careers, dating, looks, money, and how we express ourselves. So it's no surprise to add shopping to the lineup. Seeing my friend Steve walk into Nordstrom's for the store's "75% off" sale is like watching Karl Lewis take on one of his legendary sprints after the gun goes off. Steve quickly bypasses the others entering the store, makes a beeline for the best designers, deftly maneuvers in and around his fellow shoppers, and makes snap judgments about quality, what to focus on and how to maximize his time. Within minutes, his race is nearly run and he is in the lead. In fact, lesser shoppers are ready to throw in the towel by now. It's too draining, too many sale tags to plow through, and too many trips to the dressing room.

Steve and Lisa should team up for doubles sometime. One can distract the other shoppers while the other unearths the gems, like a pig ferreting out truffles. She even admits that sometimes she's in the game just for the adrenaline rush. "Shopping is more of a sport. I view it just like how my husband obsesses about the NCAA. And I like the shopping equivalent of floor seats at the Knicks game. That means I want the best. I want to win! It's competition of the visual variety!" Lisa's motto should be "Veni, Vedi, Visa: I came. I Saw. I Did a Little Shopping."

So how do you maximize your shopping experiences and play to win? Here are some strategies for maximizing your style without emptying your wallet:

1. *Access Your Inner Stylist*. Pretend you are Angelina Jolie getting ready for an awards show. Would she tolerate less than perfection? No. Why should you set your standards any lower? It might take some effort, but become your own demanding client. Have designer taste without matching finances? Forget what fashion magazines call, "Designer Looks for Less." You can do better on your own. It's all in the details.

2. *Ms. Right Place, Right Time.* Be careful at discount stores. Always know what you want from them. The truth is that some are great for "blue-collar chic" items such as Timberland boots and comfort clothes such as thermal tops. But don't try to turn hamburger into steak, if you know what I mean. Who wants to spend at least an hour digging through mostly ugly clothes to find a so-so item that looks breathtaking next to all the ugly stuff? Back at home you realize how plain it is and then have to go back to the nasty store to return it. In addition to buying only "safe" items, find out from store managers what days are "new shipment arrival" days. Thirty-six-year-old Ted from New York, an expert at keeping track of "new shipment days," finds top quality merchandise everywhere from the back room at Loehmann's to Banana Republic to Syms. Also, be careful at outlet stores. Some stores and designers make lesser quality clothing just for these stores.

3. *Target Your Opportunity.* You have got to give Target an E for effort if nothing else. Five years ago, if you had told me I'd be writing an ode to this newly crowned leader among discount stores, I'd have said you're crazy. But with its recent fashion savvy, Target now has "street cred" with the gays. We love the color, the variety, and the style. We also know that if all the gays behind Target left, the buildings would collapse. Thanks to Isaac Mizrahi, Todd Oldham, and the gay sensibility that's taken over the place, Target proves you don't have to have unlimited funds to get designer style.

4. *Window Shopping by Remote*. Before you hit the stores, prepare by channel surfing! Style Channel, with programs such as *Fashiontrance* and HGTV, help to give women affordable options for style and organization. But please don't get addicted to QVC and HSN. Next thing you know, you'll end up like thirty-three-year-old Alice from Long Island, $150 poorer and wearing cotton/poly blend denim ponchos with little flowers stitched into them. "I could cry for the time and money I spent on QVC," she told me. "I've spent hundreds of dollars during depressed moments on outfits I would run from if I saw them up close. The depression would pass but then I'd be left with some of the ugliest clothes a girl could ever have. Now I keep the credit card and phone far from the television and use the tube as educational not transactional."

5. *Know Your Salesperson*. Know your person is still the first rule of business, and knowing your salesperson should be one of your top rules for shopping. As Bobbi noted, "I need to shop where I have a one-on-one with the shop clerk or owner in a more boutique setting representational of the buyer/owner." She finds the specialty places run by gay men. She makes friends and they look out for her. They get to know her style and alert her when the perfect outfit or piece of furniture appears. Have at least a couple of places where you have a one-on-one with the owner. Get on the mailing list. In some cases, you might get discounts for holidays or your birthday, as well as get alerts for upcoming events and sales.

6. *Don't Despair, Compare.* All men are experts at comparing. We are men, and we learned how to compare everything from body parts to lunches way back in the sand box. Now we apply the "don't despair, compare" approach to shopping. Look around to find what you like and, once you have, look around again to get the best price. Remember, you can always bargain for discounts on an easily replaced button or a simple-to-clean smudge when sealing the deal. To borrow from the old saying about opera, it ain't over until the cash register rings!

7. *Let's Go Surfing Now, Everybody's Learning How.* Surf, surf, surf at online malls like www.smartbargains.com and http://www.finderguy.com, which can help you find what you are looking for without wasting time in your car speeding from mall to mall. If you are considering buying something you find online, do what my gay friends do and observe a waiting period of twenty-four hours. If you still want it after that, and you've comparison shopped, then go girl. This may be the only time some gay men show prudence in their impulsiveness. Or do what New Yorker Christel does and use the Internet as research only. "I use the Internet to research styles and prices before and after going to the store. It saves me time and money. For example, I once fell in love with this $100 sarong at a pricey boutique, however, I found the same sarong (with a matching purse!) for about $12 on bluefly.com. Of course, I ended up buying four and still saved money."

8. *Onward and Upward*. Buy something better than what you had before. Take one style step forward. Overcompensation sometimes has advantages. You develop an internal sense of needing externals to overcompensate for feelings of self-loathing. When you don't fit in as a kid, you are always looking for what's better, a better world.

9. *Use Your Points!* As Cathleen says, "I feel less guilty when I use my American Express card points, which never felt real to me anyway. Last week I traded a few thousand points for a $1500 Saks Fifth Avenue gift certificate. I didn't think twice about it, as I would have if I'd spent that." Of course, the secret is not to run up your credit card just so you can get more points. You think some sneaky gay man hasn't already thought of that angle?

10. *Use a Personal Shopper*. Sometimes, the older and busier you get, the less time you have to spend on shopping. Sadly, perhaps your gay best friend is older and busier, too. Don't you hate it when that happens? As forty-year-old Jennifer from Boston told me, "I didn't get the competitive shopping gene unfortunately. And despite the best efforts of my friend Alexander, who took me out many a Saturday for lessons in 'speed shopping,' I never did develop it. A year ago I spent way more time and a lot more money on clothes than I anticipated. So I said the hell with it. When my gay friends aren't available, I head to the personal shoppers at Neiman Marcus and Saks. I can't afford to roam around stores aimlessly."

Seven Quick and Easy Secrets When You Are Clothes Shopping

Let me leave with these quick and easy secrets from a few gay male friends of mine:

1. Buy quality, and only after trying it on, moving around and sitting down on it.

2. Go to sales of the best stores (location, location, location).

3. Each store is good for one thing.

4. Establish your signature piece.

5. Avoid "too-cutesy" clothes. A little goes a long way.

6. The only clothes to buy from e-BAY are good British imports, which are a steal.

7. A flash of sequins can glamorize anything.

14

PLASTIC SURGERY:
BOOBS, NOSE, OR NADA?

Single, searching for love, and contemplating
a physical tweak? Some advice about making
semipermanent changes.

I tried to talk Terry, a thirty-six-year-old sales executive, out
of an expensive chemical peel and laser eye job. I did this not
because they are unsafe procedures or overly costly. I did
this because I knew her motivation was boosting her sexual
allure to men. There's no doubt that chemical peels can be an
improvement, especially for overly wrinkled or acne-scarred
faces. And laser procedures might help remove wrinkles a
tad. But I'll tell you one thing about marginal cosmetic procedures. No straight man ever looked a woman over and said
to himself, "Oh my God, the fine skin around the outside
corners of her eyes is microscopically less wrinkled than it
was the last time I saw her. Damn, I want her now."

Terry, an athletic, funny, and natural blonde, looks great
the way she is, but I can understand her desire to ratchet up
her "babe" quotient. We all have that desire from time to

time (do you hear the chorus of gay men from New York's Chelsea district to San Francisco's Castro Street shouting out "Amen" in unison?). It's not surprising. If you buy in to current stereotypes, gay men often reach the shelf life on what one stylist I know calls their "parts of origin" earlier than women, so there's reason for us to know about plastic surgery early. *What's surprising to me is the number of women who want cosmetic enhancements that aren't in tandem with their goals.* These women go to great lengths to get small tweaks like microdermabrasion that most people won't even notice.

As life guru Martha Stewart would agree, improvements are a good thing, and commonplace. How many women color hair, wear makeup, and get manicures in order to boost appearance? But there's a difference between improvements that aid your goals and those that don't help or are, at worst, senseless.

Jenny, a forty-five-year-old writer, wants a facelift because she wants to look younger, but she's fifty pounds overweight. Unless the surgeon's cutting from her knees up, she isn't going to get the desired effect she wants. Someone had to step in and tell her the truth. A pulled back pinhead might make her look disproportional rather than refreshed. She's also considering liposuction on her thighs and rear end. Let's be honest about liposuction. It's for spots, not entire real estate. No doctor is going to remove half of your ass with a suction needle.

Where are the responsible medical practitioners when women like Terry and Jenny ask for help? Aren't they there to provide honest feedback? One look at Michael Jackson and I guess the answer is "not always."

I've seen too many bad touch-ups to keep my mouth shut. If they don't correlate to your goals for improvement, then what's the point? What are the typical physical enhancement goals and the best avenues for reaching them with and without surgery? Organizations like the National Board of Plastic Surgery, and websites such as www.cosmeticsupport.com, www.safecosmeticsurgery.com, and www.cosmeticsurgerynetwork.org offer guidelines for evaluating the latest procedures.

Another danger of plastic surgery is that tweaking can become addictive. Says Mary Ann, forty, "Botox is the marijuana of plastic surgery. You start with Botox. Next thing you know you're addicted, with an eye job scheduled at the doctor's earliest convenience." You start out thinking of small improvements and the next thing you know, you've got cheek implants that make you look like cartoon characters Chip n' Dale. Worse, there's enough collagen in your lips to ensure you'll never drown, a "tear trough" implant to take care of the sunken circles under the eyes, and a face shot so full of diluted botulism toxin that you'll look surprised and happy even in your sleep, at least until it wears off in about three months.

Finally, plastic surgery can be dangerous. The American Society of Anesthesiologists reports that, of the forty million anesthetics administered in the U.S. annually, there is one anesthesia-related death per 250,000. The risks are real.

Reality TV shows like *Extreme Makeover* and *Nip/Tuck* glamorize what can be costly and risky procedures. Olivia Goldsmith, author of *The First Wives Club*, died after going into an anesthesia-induced coma before getting what a friend of hers described as "a routine neck lift." Ironically, one of the characters in *The First Wives Club* is a plastic surgery addict in a desperate attempt to keep her man and career.

I have known women who wanted to get a stronger chin and ended up looking like Jay Leno. Jackie, forty-eight, got her breasts lifted and enlarged as a twentieth wedding gift to her husband only to discover he liked them the way they were. Julie, thirty-five, got liposuction on her stomach and thighs and has had to go back three times to reshape her figure due to unevenness between the liposuctioned and surrounding areas.

If you haven't known anyone personally who's disfigured herself (unfortunately, I have), then you just have to look at some perennial pop culture figures to learn that less is more.

Joan Rivers looks like she's been pulled more times than a pig at a barbecue, dipped in a combination of formaldehyde and bleach, then covered with bling-bling. She says she does this to look better on television. Maybe she means television on Mars, because my E! Channel screen shows a space alien in couture. Melanie Griffith is almost unrecognizable. I worry that if she stands next to a radiator too long she'll liquefy, we'll hear that babydoll voice whisper, "I'm melting," and someone will have to return those lips to the bee who stung them. The leaning tower of Pisa has nothing on Charlie's sexiest former angel Farrah Fawcett. Her face now leans to the right as if gravity were a horizontal force. This is the saddest story to me, as Farrah, the idol of a generation of men, would have been a beautiful older woman. Now her face is a totally stretched, lopsided mask. On the male side, there's Burt Reynolds, once the smoldering Smokey from *Smokey and the Bandit*. After what appear to be numerous facelifts, eye jobs, and hair pieces, I want to take a fireman's hose and spray Burt Reynolds until the hair comes off, the fake tan dissolves, and what's left of the real man reappears. I don't even know where to begin to describe the horrors of now unrecognizable stars like Mickey Rourke and Axl Rose.

With the exception of Joan Rivers, who ironically makes a living commenting on how bad other people look, my point is not to excoriate these women or men. My point is to help you make smarter decisions about what you do to fix yourself up, and why.

I've never met a straight man that didn't want to at least recognize his woman after any procedure. The plastic surgery horror stories are the ones where the people look fundamentally changed afterwards. You don't want that. If I have to, I'll hurl myself in front of the operating room door to stop you from doing that. If I get run over by an overzealous candy striper pushing the rollaway bed, then I consider it essential bravery in a gay best friend's line of duty.

Many women would be surprised that men don't want their women to be so radically different. Linda, a thirty-year-old from Massachusetts, said recently, "I am so sad that Pamela Anderson had her breast implants restored. I cheered when she had them taken out. I felt like she buckled to men's desires." But my straight friend Mike's opinion was similar to many I heard. He said, "It honestly didn't matter to me. She's a babe either way, with or without the boobs. The way she carries herself and her outrageousness are much bigger turn-ons than the relative size of her chest. In fact, they kind of look fake and too hard to touch now."

Ken, a thirty-one-year-old stockbroker in Washington,

says, "Being trim and athletic is important to me, but many women spend time on their hair, debating cosmetic surgery, and getting new boobs, and yet avoid just staying trim."

Sometimes, straight men just want you to have long hair. Whether or not you want to have long hair is another matter. But my point is you have to consider the source. If you are thinking about getting a cosmetic procedure, take this advice from your gay best friend:

1. *Consider Less Risky Options First.* What is it that you want to do? Look better for yourself, for other women, for men, or for some combination of these? There are an increasing number of minor, minimally invasive procedures that are less costly, risky, and time consuming. But they can positively alter your appearance. Procedures such as brow shaping (an art if there ever were one), fat injections, and laser surgery make a difference. There are even safer ways to tan, including a spray with atomized tanning solution. Just make sure you avoid that awful, orange, overtanned look. It might not be harmful to the skin, but it's hell on the eyes, let me tell you. My point is this: think twice before risky, invasive procedures. Are the risks really worth it?

2. *Try a Shot of Confidence First.* Before getting filled with silicone, try a shot of confidence to boost your attitude before you boost your bust. It worked for Linda, a thirty-four-year-old chef in Pennsylvania. "I always wanted big breasts, even since I was little. I talked it

over with my friend Hank and my girlfriends, and implants just seemed scary to me. Hank helped me make
the most of my look instead. I am fairly tall, so he
helped me see that it's cool to be slim and willowy,
even if I do have a fairly flat chest. Clothes fit well on
me. I didn't hide my body quite so much. When I
walked, I started to think of myself as a dancer. Seeing
myself in a different light that way helped my confidence tremendously."

3. *Sometimes Less Is More.* Initially, thirty-two-year-old
store manager Lisa felt like she owed it to men to have
big boobs. "They hurt my back and made me feel awkward," she says. After some soul-searching, she reduced her DD bust size to a C and felt more confident.
She was surprised that guys didn't even notice, but she
sure did. Her clothes fit (a huge relief!) and she could
now feel great in lingerie. Armed with Victoria's Secret
teddies and silky lingerie and her new attitude, she was
definitely noticed more by her boyfriend Ken. "I think
of how I could have done it sooner, but at least they're
better now."

4. *Align Your Plans with Your Goal.* Know your goal, and
make well-thought-out choices accordingly. If you are
married or partnered to a man, then get his honest
thoughts before you make up your mind after looking
at twenty-year-old anorexic genetic mutants parading
in *Vogue* or feeling paranoid as you watch your guy
glance at the Spice Channel. If some part of you has
bothered you for years and you just want it fixed for

yourself, knowing full well that Moses will not part the Red Sea out of sheer amazement when he sees you next, then go for it.

5. *Remember That Surgery Is Hit or Miss.* Don't underestimate the "miss" part of this sentence. When you gamble you have to be willing to lose. Many types of surgery, like facelifts, are a gamble despite the doctors who will tell you exactly how you'll look afterward. You never gamble if you can't afford to lose so pick reputable people to help you. This is no time to hit the bargain bins of medicine, not when your valuable face and body are involved. For example, if you are choosing a doctor, make sure he's certified by the American Board of Plastic Surgery.

6. *Wait It Out, Sister!* When stem cell technology is improved (say in about ten years' time), women who underwent the knife and aren't happy about it will be ticked off when they look back and see that, if they had waited, better results could have been theirs much more easily. Stem cells will be injected directly into the face and will encourage the formation of collagen and make the cells in the face regrow. The result, according to some experts, will be fresh new faces without scarring and other complications.

7. *Don't Overdo.* Getting that lush full look for your lips doesn't mean Barbara Hershey in *Beaches*. Bigger boobs don't mean Pamela Anderson redux, in one of her Dolly Parton phases (Pamela makes implant de-

posits and withdrawals as if her body is a bank. Do her boobs have zippers? Makes you wonder). Face procedures should refresh, not make you a candidate for the witness protection program.

8. *Focus on Weight and Skin First*. For your health and for how men see you, focus on your weight and skin first. When it comes to skincare, Britney Spears and followers, I am talking to you! Take care of your skin now. Throw the tanning bed off your tour bus. As for weight management, the old adage is that, as you age, you save either your ass or your face. I don't think this is true! What kind of a *Sophie's Choice* is this for women to make? I think this popular notion was an excuse started by a former beauty queen who, after hitting forty and having it hit back, reached for the Ding Dongs and never looked back. Save both as best you can.

9. *Research, Research, Research*. This is your face and body we're talking about changing. This isn't getting a fashionable new nail tip design or even a new hairdo. No one has a right to be critical of those who make cosmetic changes. It is a personal decision, but one that needs to be researched very carefully. But don't be secret about it. Let friends know. Be honest with the medical people about medications you are taking as well as other potential mitigating factors such as allergies. Be careful. You could have allergies or other conditions you might not be aware of that will affect the anesthesia, sometimes the most dangerous element of plastic surgery. Tell your anesthesiologist everything!

He'll be your new best friend right before any procedure you'll have. Welcome their input and comments.
Factor in three steps: 1) research with medical experts,
2) feedback from those who you (honestly) might be
doing it for, such as the man in your life, and 3) your
gay best friend, who will quiz you to make sure you
completed steps #1 and # 2, as well as put in his own
two cents. But ultimately the decision is yours.

10. *You Are Beautiful As Is*. Enhancements are great. But
they only enhance beauty; they don't create it. You are
the only one who can really make yourself feel beautiful. That comes from you and you alone, not society,
your friends, or your man. Remember that the only acceptable male response to anything you do, whether it's
for yourself or for him, is "You were beautiful before,
and now you're even more beautiful."

15

AWAKENING THE INTERIOR DESIGNER WITHIN

Don't follow your mother off the home decoration cliff!

Most species rely on their parents to learn how to survive in the world. I watch Animal Planet. I know how this works. Many species bond with their young and separate later in the life cycle, with the kids carrying forth traits of the parents. Part of this is genetic and perfectly normal. But when it comes to home decoration, part of it is just bad habits that won't die! The young might require immersion in behavior modification therapy in order lose the bad traits and cultivate the beautiful ones.

What are a few bad habits that lead women to follow their mothers over the home decorating cliff?

- A formal dining room or living room that you never use.

- Beautiful things that you hide, such as china and silver.

- Forty teddy bears and yet you are just thirty-seven. As a general rule, you should have fewer visible teddy bears than the number of your age. In fact, no more than three.

Your mother has or had her style. You need to find yours. Your first three apartments, including the college dorm and off-campus housing abode, don't count. It's just assumed that you went with home décor that was affordable and familiar to the person whose name was on the MasterCard, probably your mother. Of course, as you are getting started in the world, you have to live with whatever décor you inherited. But there comes a point when you wake up, look around, and hold my hand for support as you declare loudly:

- "I cannot stand flowered curtains one more minute!"

- "I do not like knickknacks and figurines on every shelf. I will not be Laura from *The Glass Menagerie.*"

- "I do not understand the need for bedspread ruffles, therefore I eschew them!"

- "I am a bold young woman and I must have bold colors around me. Good-bye, pink pastel!"

Your very independence in the world depends on this crucial step. Think of getting tips to awaken your inner designer and find your own style as an essential rite of passage for every girl.

"I was raised in the Midwest and my mom's sense of style was so muted," says Lisa, a thirty-year-old creative designer in Virginia. To give you an example, we had a huge fireplace with a boar's head over it. So when I started to develop my own personal style, my goal was simplicity. Or, at the very least, no more dead animals in the living room."

Lisa and her husband, Paul, are two of my close friends. Over martinis one night when she had the evening off from her newborn, we had a rare, sacred gay boyfriend date. I shared with her a few stories from my research with women. At crucial jointures in their lives, all of these women had gay men who acted like the proverbial fairy godfathers of style:

"My gay friend Tom walked into to my house and said, 'No, no, no,' " says Suzanne, a thirty-four-year-old public relations professional in New Jersey. "He wasn't being mean, he was using the gay boyfriend shorthand to help me reinvent my living space because he knew I wasn't happy with it. In thirty minutes he had rearranged the living room and dining room so that there was more space, and the living room was centered around my fireplace, as it should have been from the start. There is something about the way he helped me visualize it—he didn't just make suggestions, my family had done that—he actually talked to me in visual terms, almost like painting a picture. I trust his judgment like no one else's. I have seen his home and how he moves into places and reinvents them but always incorporating them into his own. I didn't want to hire a designer to come in and just tell me what I wanted to hear."

"I grew up with money but sadly, we had the gaudiest types of furniture you can imagine," says Karen, a twenty-eight-year-old retail clerk in Atlanta. "It cost a lot, and our house was humongous, like many houses are in Atlanta. But it wasn't good stuff. My gay friend helped me to see what was real quality as opposed to just expensive crap."

"My friend Jerry the designer helped me decorate my first apartment. I remember being amazed at how he took fabrics and somehow created window treatments," says Mary, a twenty-nine-year-old graduate student in New York. "I was under the impression you had to have big bucks to be creative at home. In my mind, home style was something I'd get to after my kids were in junior high school and I had some time and (hopefully) money on my hands. What Jerry did with $300 and his own creativity was miraculous."

After years of ignoring her home décor in favor of the going-out-all-the-time New York City lifestyle, Cathleen decided to hire someone to help her. "After years of not focusing on my place, it didn't cross my mind that I even had home style. Everything was a mishmash of old and new, good and bad. I spent a couple of weekends looking around for new furniture and then just threw my hands in the air. So I hired a gay decorator and we went shopping together. After spending a day together he said, 'You know exactly what you like, you just don't know how to find it.' He made me realize that I had a style. This is the legacy of my mother. I thought that I didn't have the confidence and skills to put different pieces together."

So let's address the age-old question: Is there a gay designer gene? Yes, but not all gay men have it. Pay attention to the ones who do. They can make an amazing difference in the way you feel about your living space, helping you turn it into a home that reflects the real you.

So where does gay style come from? Based on gay designers I've known, I'd say it's often the result of creativity combined with overcompensation. The lesson to be learned from overcompensation is that, while often draining, the results in your home are always good.

Why do gay men have such a passion for design? One theory is that gay men and lesbians sometimes have great passion for and engage in activities that they were interested in, but denied as children. For gay men, perhaps design was "sissy stuff." For some lesbians, maybe an interest in car or home repairs led to remarks like, "It's not ladylike to change the oil."

Whatever the reason, no one can deny that the home design industry would collapse if you extracted all the gay men from it. Whether it's helping you find or awaken your style or get you out of the home décor rut you were raised in, gay designers can help you.

"I see a lot of women trapped in a given style, complete with objects and furniture, and they don't know how to extricate," says William McGinn of William McGinn Interior Design in Manhattan. "It's usually out of guilt, something that belonged to her mother. The solution for women in this position is to make the style, object, or furniture their own. Stain the furniture or flooring. If it's a cabinet, light the interior and fill it with the things that you love, and not the old china you hold onto out of guilt."

McGinn has many female clients and adds, "Women who consult a gay man are typically more into being creative than in doing the 'right' thing, or the thing they feel they are expected to do. The gay man is coming from outside the box, because obviously we're not in the box," McGinn says with a laugh. "Though it's a stereotype that every gay man has great taste, more than likely we're able to see the sex appeal in the solution. Men are very visual."

Whether you decide to consult with a designer, milk your gay best friend for all he's worth in the home department, or experiment on your own, keep these guidelines in mind as you explore and awaken your inner designer:

1. *Color Changes Everything.* Life isn't black and white, right? So don't be a black-and-white girl in this colorful world. The gay designers I know are colorful individuals with different styles, but they agree on one thing. If you are new to design and on a budget but still want to experiment with home design, the biggest bang for your buck is a can of paint.

2. *Your Space Needs to Reflect You.* At different stages of your life, you will have different amounts of space. When you start out, usually you have less. It's easy to think there's not much you can do with it. Wrong! The space will dictate what you can do with it, for instance how much and what you want to focus on first. But most importantly, before you start planning, figure out what are you all about. Your home should reflect that, whether it's a studio apartment or a mansion.

3. *Don't Blend in. Stand Out!* Who better than a gay man knows the strong pull in our society for all of us to blend in? How boring! Who wants to do that? Obviously, lots of people do, but not you. It's my job to show you how much more fun and interesting it is to stand out. One way your home can stand out is by contrasting fabrics, styles, and colors until you have a space that is as unique as you are.

4. *Set the Stage.* When you are setting up your space, make sure to set the stage by focusing on backgrounds as much as you do furniture, rugs, and other central aspects of your space. Backgrounds include details such as window treatments and floor trim that add subtle flavor and context to your home.

5. *Single? Now Is Your Time to Experiment!* If it's your first real apartment, or you find yourself living alone for any number of reasons, you might not get another chance to experiment so freely to find your style. So be bold! Play with color, fabric, and design before you are married with kids or settled down with a partner with whom you'll make joint decisions.

6. *Don't Throw the Mother Out with the Bathwater.* Sometimes women run so hard from their mother's style that they throw the proverbial baby out with the bathwater. In other words, they dismiss all aspects of the style in which they were raised. Fight this. It can actually inhibit you from finding your own style, which might include elements of mom's along with new elements. For

example, one woman I know likes the traditional style she was raised in, peppered with contemporary elements.

7. *Clutter Is a Spiritual Issue.* A few years ago, my friend Bonnie was in a slump. She was sitting at home, obsessed over a recently ended relationship with a younger man, uncertain about her life's direction, and generally not a happy camper. Her apartment reflected this sad state of affairs. The makeup counter was now in the kitchen next to the coffee pot. Why? Apparently, there'd been a hostile takeover of the bathroom by hosiery, plants, and hair care products. Her living room resembled a variety store. Looking for bobby pins, magazines, winter clothes still displayed in the spring, or a month's worth of mail? Look no further than her coffee table. Whatever the opposite of feng shui is, that's what Bonnie's place resembled. My inner gay Buddha took her hand and said to her, "Clutter is a spiritual issue. Clear your mind and clean your house."

8. *Make Your Home Man-Friendly.* Lest you think gay style is about giving you license to create a girly pink lair with estrogen-scented candles wafting through the air, think again! I want you and your guy to be comfortable. Limit the flowers and the fragrances. Did you know that perfume-scented candles are Kryptonite for some straight men? Bear in mind (no pun intended) that if you are going for "little girl appeal," he'd much rather have you in a Catholic schoolgirl miniskirt uniform than see you surrounded by a backdrop of mangy

cotton animals with beady glass eyes. There's an old adage that the way to a man's heart is through his stomach. But the number one way to his heart is through electronics! Get decent ones. This means, at minimum, that you should buy the biggest flat screen television that you can afford. Second is comfort. Make sure that he has furniture that he can sink into and relax. Nothing is worse than trying to relax in one of those rickety, hard, wooden chairs that look great in museums but were clearly not made for a guy's—or anyone's—comfort.

9. *Don't Be Afraid to Raise Your Hand and Ask for Help.* Help will allow you to clarify your style, not lose it. Help can be everything from magazines to hiring a designer if you can afford it. Often gay men will just hire. The gay men I know who can afford it value their time enough and want to get the job done right enough that they won't think twice about getting design help. Gay men appreciate simplification—life is tough enough. As one friend of mine said, "There are some problems you can solve with money, so why not?"

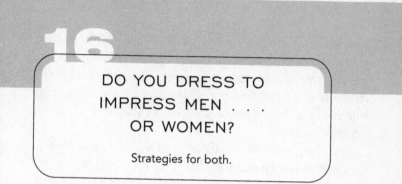

16

DO YOU DRESS TO IMPRESS MEN . . . OR WOMEN?

Strategies for both.

There are two kinds of women. There are women who dress to impress other women, and women who dress for men. (Actually, there are three if you count nudists, but we'll skip them for now.)

I have spent many a Saturday afternoon with both types of women. Like all good consultants, I have devised fool-proof strategies for both types of "clients" to maximize their time and money to achieve their dressing goals. Now if only I got paid.

Does dressing even matter anymore? Will you be judged for style and clothing, or for what you have to say and what's in your heart? Hopefully we'll all be judged more for the latter than we will for the merely superficial. But the old adage, "You never get a second chance to make a first impression" holds true. Most opinions are formed within the first few seconds of meeting. Presentation is crucial. What else can you assess about someone in the amount of time we are given? You cannot judge someone's deep well of inner thoughts in a brief meeting. Often you cannot even judge someone's actions without knowing all the facts. So we go by what we see.

One thing you can say about gay men. We know how to vary our wardrobe and style based on the situation, setting, and goal. Usually we know we have to play the game at work and wear what's appropriate, with just a little extra flair. It's even more important for some gay men to dress well at work since we have a need to overcompensate. Once we're on our own time, it's important for us to express ourselves. One of the ways we do this is through what we wear. Straight men seem perfectly comfortable wearing the same suit they wore to work out for a night on the town. Not so for many gay men. If we're going out with friends or on a date that night, we want to lose the formal suit in favor of our cool, new party shirt. We know that other gay men will appreciate the effort.

If you are a woman who dresses to impress other women, you feel the same way. We both know that we're faced with meeting impossibly high standards all the time. We just accept it as a fact of life. That's why I am with you at Neiman Marcus, Nordstrom's, and high-end boutiques, concerned about fabric, color, flattering line, and, of course, shoes. Lunch is an essential element of our time together, and it's best in a restaurant worthy of your extensive purchases. Somehow, a Big Mac and fries ordered from the drive-through squawk box doesn't reflect the thought that we've both put into the day.

"My gay friends understand why my entire wardrobe is sorted out by color, season, and fabric," says Peggy, twenty-eight-year-old fundraiser who divides her time between the Hamptons and New York City. Peggy thinks of herself as a woman who dresses to impress other women. "I know my audience. Certain kinds of women and gay men are the only ones who notice the details, which I find fun. They notice the style, the history, and the coordination of accessories."

Some of the essentials for dressing to impress other women include:

1. *Play Up Accessories.* Women appreciate the details. So have fun with mixing and matching the accessories. Many women and gay men like to express their individuality through their clothes, but women have so many more options. So have fun with the details since you can!

2. *Know When to Tone It Down.* "Be aware that the woman you are going to meet might be competitive," says Rachel, a twenty-eight-year-old editor. "I was on a job interview with an older woman in my industry. I'm young, blond, and slim, and the last thing I want to do is remind her of the girl who ran off with her husband or makes her feel frumpy every day."

3. *Pay Attention to Details.* This really applies if it's a professional setting. "When I am conducting an interview, I always notice the details of how someone is dressed," says Meg, a thirty-eight-year-old director of human resources. "If a woman walks in with rips in her panty-

hose or scuffed up shoes, I wonder how much she cares about the details of her work. One woman walked in and was a total mess. She was applying for a job in our advertising department. I felt like asking her if she saw any irony in that statement. After all, when you are interviewing, you are your own ad."

If you are a woman who dresses to impress men, our Saturday shopping excursion is relatively quick. The whole spree takes no more than an hour, or however long the Gap clerk requires to ring up your sleeveless T-shirts, halter-tops, simple short skirts, airy dresses, and jeans. Lunch is optional after this type of retail outing. In fact, I consider myself lucky if I get a Whopper thrown at me by the drive-thru clerk, as you speed home. Men like casual dress on women, but make sure it's flattering casual, enough so that the clothes tell him to treat you like the hottie you are. I am sure it was a straight man who came up with the saying, "If she's wearing baggy pants, call her a man. If she's wearing a dress, call her a cab."

"I dress for men a little more," says thirty-five-year-old Jeannine. "It becomes this game for me. How much of my bra can I show under my shirt to titillate? Of course, it has to be a sexy, lacy black bra. And the goal is to show only a hint, as if it's unplanned."

Melissa adds, "When I dress to impress men, my blouse is lower cut. I 'show the twins,' as my gay friend Brian describes them. I wear a skirt that flatters my legs. I wear my favorite perfume to smell good."

What are the essentials for dressing to impress straight men?

1. *Accentuate the Positive.* Put your best foot forward, preferably in a "come-do-me" Manolo Blahnik pump. Accentuate your sexiest features, whether it's your legs, chest, eyes, or other areas.

2. *Casual Is Sexy, Overdone Is Not.* Straight men prefer a woman who looks casual vs. overdone any day. "Sometimes when my girlfriend is all dressed up, I feel like she's lacquered," says Neil, a thirty-two-year-old marketer in Chicago. "Man, she paints it on with the makeup and sprays her hair until it's hard as a frickin' rock. She looks good, but I just want to get her home, where she can be simple and sexy again."

3. *Your Inside Is as Important as Your Outside.* Of course, what I mean is that your heart and soul are what's most important. But sexy lingerie, especially in black or red, can make your heart and soul really sparkle, don't you think? From his point of view, the beautiful dress you're wearing is only a tease for what's underneath, unless of course you are in the timeless LBD (Little Black Dress), in which case you can never go wrong.

17

FORGET THE FIVE POUNDS YOU'VE BEEN TRYING TO LOSE FOR TEN YEARS

Hint: It's not what's standing between you and the life of your dreams!

"I am almost ready to date again. I can feel it. I just need to lose five to ten pounds and I'll be ready to conquer the world," my friend Bonnie told me in 1989. And 1992. Again in 1995. And as recently as last year. Bonnie has a pixie hairstyle, Tina Turner legs, and she looks hot in a miniskirt.

Of course, you'll never know this because she's living her life like a cloistered nun.

She's fallen victim to the "My life can start as soon as I lose five to ten pounds" syndrome that's been know to strike otherwise attractive urban women.

Your mother will tell you to eat less. Your girlfriends will advise one senseless diet after the next. Your boyfriend will say he doesn't care (he might even be telling the truth). But let me give you the best advice of all: get over yourself.

Because a few pounds, a bad hairstyle, or three more years

to "process" that awful six-month relationship are not what's keeping you down. You are keeping you down, and creating myths about your life to foster your complacency. I want you to conquer the myths that are keeping you down with stories from women who stopped waiting and started living.

What are a few of these myths?

You have to lose weight before you can date. You aren't smart enough to compete at work. A fabulous life is a shallow life. You are too old (or too young). You have to live out the dreams your parents had or have for you. You can't be happy on your own.

Let's deal with each one from your gay boyfriend's perspective:

MYTH #1. YOU HAVE TO LOSE WEIGHT BEFORE YOU CAN DATE. The truth is that you have to feel good about yourself to have a decent dating life. Far be it for a gay man to tell you that fat girls have an easy time of it in the dating world. We have to deal with plenty of judgments from other men and a society that still dictates you can never be too rich or too thin. The downside for some women and gay men is that weight becomes an obsession that they cannot evaluate objectively. If I had a dime for all the people I know who look great but insist they're fat, I'd be rich enough to go to Canyon Ranch for a month. Sometimes it's a gift to be able to see others' struggles so clearly. It was for Suzanne, who told me, "In some ways, my gay friends actually foster the myth that weight loss matters. In other ways, I learned from what I saw as their mistakes. I saw them struggle with their own brutal myths such as 'their dates must meet physical standards that they could never approach themselves.' In a weird way it actually helped lessen my feeling that weight was holding me back. It made me seek a partner who was reasonable in his requirements."

The other truth is that I have never met a woman or gay man whose life drastically changed after losing a few pounds. Now I am not talking about twenty pounds or more. Those kinds of weight loss can alter your appearance drastically. But you can't make those kinds of changes to your appearance *expecting* others to view or treat you differently. Next time you diet to keep your guy happy, just remember that it's more important to have a boyfriend who cares when you feel bad about yourself than a boyfriend who's the cause of it.

MYTH #2. YOU AREN'T SMART ENOUGH TO RUN YOUR LIFE OR COMPETE AT WORK. Our society still panders to outdated stereotypes and sex roles. Gay men fight homophobia and "lavender ceilings" at work. Women must overcome the absurd notion that the most important thing they can be is cute. You have to overcome many hurdles about money, taking care of yourselves, and feeling entitled to leadership positions at work.

MYTH #3. A FABULOUS LIFE IS A SHALLOW LIFE. I hate the myth that fabulous means shallow. Since gay men get labeled "fabulous," and the word is, in fact, part of the title of this book, I want to clarify it. *True fabulousness is not shallow. It doesn't seek to put down others or be overly competitive. It's cultivating the best of everything and the best in others and ourselves.* That's it. "I was working at a fabulous PR agency promoting food and wine to the upper crust," says Suzanne. "I was surrounded by the shallowest people. I was miserable, my confidence was sinking to an all time low. I felt like a big nothing next to the company I was keeping. My gay friend Mike gave me a 'Cher in *Moonstruck* snap-out-of-it moment' slap in the face. 'Why are you doubting yourself?' he asked. 'You think you have to be as "fabulous" as these idiots. But it's all a game, sweetie. Don't get too caught up in it, because so much of it is b.s.' " Of course, Mike was referring to the competition, the insincerity, the backstabbing—all dressed up and towering in their tuxedos and sequined gowns. That's not the real fabulous. The real fabulous is quality, pure and simple. And there's always room for more of it and more truly fabulous people.

MYTH #4. YOU ARE TOO OLD (OR TOO YOUNG). Whether we admit it to ourselves or not, we face a cultural tidal wave of ageism. I've seen far too many women "check out" of life fearing ridicule or judgment. I've decided to adopt Sharon Stone's basic instincts when it comes to aging. As she said recently, "If they don't dig me because I'm over forty, then guess what? I'll be fabulous and creative over here, and when they catch up with that . . . you call me!" Sharon has come through marriage, motherhood, illness, divorce, and some career cooling and landed in a better place. Her ego and confidence have not been blunted. Don't let yours get blunted, either.

MYTH #5. YOU HAVE TO LIVE OUT THE DREAMS YOUR PARENTS HAD OR HAVE FOR YOU. If I had lived out the dreams my parents had for me, I'd be a married, successful doctor living in suburban Virginia right now. Of course, they wanted me to be happy. They just had fairly rigid ideas of what that meant. In my case, it meant straight. When my parents were growing up, gay men were sad, lonely, and ostracized people. Of course, anyone who's spent a weekend with urban gay men knows that lonely and ostracized hardly apply. Once you get older you realize that their parents instilled those ideas about success in their heads, too. Parents pass down their dreams, whether consciously or unconsciously, to their kids. But at the end of the day, it's your life and you have to be true to yourself.

MYTH #6. YOU CAN'T BE HAPPY ON YOUR OWN. Recently, I eavesdropped on a conversation between a gay man and his female friend at Starbucks. She said, "I just feel like my happiness is dependent on Mike. We've been seeing each other for a year now." The gay guy turned toward her and said, "Your feelings are correct, but honey, your facts are all wrong." I couldn't have said it better myself. I would have added, "You can be happy on your own. In fact, you can only be happy on your own." Nothing can bring you peace but yourself. For the modern girl, "nothing" includes boys, money, shoes, and did I mention boys? As Cathleen says, "A lot of women are still in Prince Charming mode. They think a prince is coming to take care of them, and that limits how seriously they take their work and lives, how they compete, and how they affect the relationships they are in because they can't look at them realistically." Helen Gurley Brown, former editor of *Cosmopolitan*, coined the term "mouseburger" to describe women who feel incomplete, timid, and empty without a man. If you feel like a "mouseburger," you have to work on your self-esteem. No one else can do it. Remember, I want to see you blossom with or without that special someone.

18

ANNIE, GET YOUR POWER DRILL!

Why you should access your inner lesbian and make those repairs yourself, plus tips on achieving gay style without emptying that Fendi purse.

A couple of women told me that going into Home Depot alone prompted the same kind of emotional response they experienced on their first trip to the gynecologist. They experienced the same fear of the unknown, scary sense of adventure, and wariness of metal objects.

How can you develop your own sense of style without flying off to Paris or Rome for a year? Without donning flannel and setting up house with a mullet-haired woman named Stan? How can you learn to handle basic home care procedures yourself, without feeling totally helpless? What are the best ways to get in touch with your inner home style Goddess?

I have spoken with many gay designers and straight women who've carved out their own style from a block of wood from Lowe's Home Center. How did they afford and complete home repairs and upgrades without help from one of their dumb ex-boyfriends?

Repeat after me: "I can be self-reliant in these matters." You don't want to have to rely on a man to caulk your tub or fix your faucet. Believe me, the cost of dependence on him is far higher than either learning how to do it yourself or hiring a plumber. At least a plumber won't get away with forgetting your anniversary or not taking you out on a proper date just because he knows his way around your pipes. If the only thing he knows how to do well is screw a nut onto a bolt, then you should bolt, not look back, and refuse to call him for household emergencies.

When it comes to home repair, sometimes we all want to follow the 17th-century Samurai Manual, which says, "When faced with a crisis, put a little spittle on each earlobe and exhale deeply through the nose. Then break a chopstick. All nervousness will disappear instantly. This is a secret matter."

But is breaking a chopstick really going to help when you accidentally pull the towel rack out of the bathroom wall, leaving a dusty trail of plaster in its wake? No. If you are single and haven't prepared yourself for small emergencies like these, you may feel the urge to "drink and dial" an old boyfriend for assistance. All of a sudden, you want the man to just come and take care of everything. Let's be clear. It's security and comfort you want, not him.

You can always call your gay boyfriend, but if for some reason he's unavailable when you call, consider these options to fortify yourself as Ms. Home Girl who can manage her own place, rather than Miss Dependent:

1. *Security and Comfort Are Learned Behaviors.* Get over the misconception that you can't fix things. Of course you can. Even if you are a traditional woman who has shied from home or car repair, the truth is that you fix things all the time. You fix problems at home, at work, and for the people in your life. Some things are easy and instinctive for you to fix. Some things you have to study and learn.

2. *Get the Right Tools, Girl!* And no, not *that* kind. Get your mind out of the gutter. I am talking about real tools that you'll need to handle basic repairs. Nowadays, the great news is that you don't need to borrow some dumb man's old rusted tool kit that he probably inherited from his father. How can a stylish, cool girl like you be expected to manhandle a huge, oafish metal toolkit from 1968? You can't. You need tools for you. One option is to visit www.lyndalyday.com for a wide selection of stylish and handy tools designed for women. Lynda is rapidly becoming like Martha Stewarts' little sister in the home design arena. In addition to tools, she offers handy instructions from the handy gal's perspective on her television show.

3. *WD-40 and Duct Tape Are Your Friends.* When I was moving into my home, a wise repairman told me, "Here's a secret. Bottom line, you really only need five tools at all times: WD-40, duct tape, hammer, nail, and screw. If it doesn't move and it should, use WD-40. If it moves and shouldn't, use the tape. If it falls out or needs to be put in, use the hammer and nails and pound

it. Or, if it requires firmer placement, screw it." Of course, using duct tape on everything might make you eligible for the trailer park, but otherwise, the advice is sound for simple fixes.

4. *"Dating" Your Contractors.* Of course, you cannot handle all home-related jobs yourself. For the big ones, you need to hire a contractor. Finding a reliable, affordable contractor who does quality work is harder than finding a husband. You want the same traits you require in mate, to be sure. He must be reliable, honest, communicative, and competent. When you are interviewing contractors, imagine you are on a date and really scrutinize him. The truth is, if you are having him build or do major repairs on your home, you'll be spending a lot of time with him, so it's important to clarify your expectations upfront and find someone compatible.

5. *Help Is a Click Away.* Thankfully, there are many free websites that offer helpful information about home repair. Visit sites like www.homedepot.com, www.lowes.com, and www.ikea.com for home planning tools and tips as well as online ordering. The National Association of the Remodeling Industry (www.nair.orgoffers) tips on selecting a contractor for home improvement. The National Association of Home Builders (www.nahb.com) offers resources and advice on planning and starting a remodeling project. Visit www.homegain.com. Home Gain's interactive Home Sale Maximizer estimates the payback on improvements taken in advance of a home sale.

6. *Ax Your Ex and Do It Yourself.* Don't rely on exes and bad boyfriends to help you fix your place. The cost to your pride might just be too high. Twenty-nine-year-old Maria found that out. "Anthony and I lived together for two hellish years, and I'd say the only thing he really did well was renovate the place. He was handy. But he was also lazy, mooching, and uncaring, too. I was ready to let the relationship go, but stayed for an additional year because I was scared of taking care of the house. I can't believe I did that." Maria learned that other men, including her gay boyfriends and straight male friends, were happy to help her at home, or at least point her to the right professional. Unlike Anthony, they were even patient and willing to teach her so she could learn how to fix a few things herself.

7. *Take It Step-by-Step.* Thank God for shows with fabulous gay style gurus like Robert Verdi, the current cohost of *Surprise by Design* on the Discovery Channel. They provide step-by-step guides for each project. The ladder to home fabulousness is climbed rung by rung as you learn how to customize rugs, lamps, and furniture. There's even a website for *Surprise by Design*'s step-by-step instructions. Visit http://dsc.discovery.com and start climbing!

8. *When in Doubt, Ty One On.* In case you don't know who he is, Ty Pennington is the sexy, lanky, blond carpenter host of several televised home-makeover shows. He provides home repair secrets that are affordable and easy, if transforming a stick of bamboo into a double

bed doesn't intimidate you. It doesn't matter if it does. He's gorgeous. He's our "home repair boyfriend." I'd listen to Ty read the Yellow Pages. With his low-riding tool belt and sarcastic manner, he comes across as Mr. Everyman, but every man doesn't look like this. If just one of his home repair tips rubs off on you during each show, it's time well spent. The stuff he paints, designs, builds, and finds is amazing and has won him a legion of straight and gay fans. The only problem with this handy "metrosexual carpenter-model" is not sharing the spaces he creates with him.

19

HOW TO USE YOUR SEX APPEAL AT WORK

Why *Ally McBeal* is so Ally McOver—and wearing a short skirt at the office doesn't make you a postfeminist pariah.

For years, I have watched my female friends go through gender identity crisis after identity crisis in corporate hallways and boardrooms.

I have heard the same questions since the 80s. Am I still a woman at work? Or am I a sexless fembot, submerging my femininity in a man's world from 9 to 5 in order to placate some tired old patriarchal model? Do I lose my feminine wiles the minute I put on that restricting Talbot's two-piece working-girl suit with the ruffled shirt laced halfway up my neck?

I say, "To hell with all of that." Be a woman, for God's sake.

I am not suggesting that you turn into Alexis Carrington Colby. Or even *Sex and The Single Girl*'s Helen Gurley Brown. I'm just saying that women who try to act and dress like men at work aren't furthering the feminist cause. They're just adding more idiots to the office pool.

Anyone who's seen *The Apprentice* knows that there's a line between being a feminine professional and a harlot. It's not a line you want to cross. But how happy can you be if you suppress who you are for the majority of the day?

"In order to succeed at my investment firm, I thought I had to act and dress like a good ole boy to break into the old boy network," says Christiane, thirty-four. "I dressed in conservative blues and gray suits and white blouses with little mini string ties until I found out that my nickname was 'Mannish Woman.' I started walking with hunched-over purpose like two of our male partners, and I yelled at the secretaries just to prove I was tough. I felt like such a phony, and I found it harder and harder to reconcile the mannish woman I'd become during the day with the woman I really was, who only got about two hours a day to show her face. I looked around me at all the harried superwomen juggling their careers, kids, and husbands. I decided that doing a good job was the only thing I owed the firm. Life was pressured enough. I didn't have to add to it by being someone I wasn't. In the spirit of full disclosure, I should add that this very hot man started working at the firm on my floor. As if the mannish woman comment wasn't enough impetus, that really did it! I changed my professional wardrobe to be professional but feminine, acted more friendly to everyone, and, within three weeks, struck a conversation with my attractive colleague that's led to a series of great dates."

You think gay men don't have to deal with identity crises at work? Of course we do. We must balance fitting in to our work environments with fear of reprisal from our gay peers. We'll get kicked out of the gay clubhouse if we don't at least attempt to be a little more cutting edge than our straight counterparts. As twenty-eight-year-old lawyer Rob says, "It rubs me the wrong way to feel I must dress like all the other guys in order to be taken seriously. I don't want to wear dark blue and gray all the time. I'm gay, not glum." It's not like he's wearing mesh knit tops to the office. No, he's kept the tailors at Prada and Armani busy finding a look and fit that suits him and work.

Let me give you some objective gay male advice on how to be yourself and queen of the workplace at the same time:

1. *If You Can't Beat Them, Join Them.* There are two professional approaches: 1) meritocracy and 2) sex sells. "Knowing that the old boy network is still alive in some places, I will at times be the cute young chick," says Sarah, a thirty-four-year-old high-tech sales executive. "I don't cross the line of bad behavior, but I am in sales, so I have to work it. So what if adopting a more flirtatious attitude helps me seal a deal? I am savvy enough to use it without letting it define me." Of course, we all wish the world worked on a meritocracy basis. It doesn't. Sometimes we are judged on superficial characteristics such as race, gender, age, sexual orientation, and plain likeability. They play a big role in how we progress in our careers. Each of us must decide how best to overcome what others might see as limitations, as well as figure out how to put our best assets up front to compete. The trick is doing this without com-

promising yourself or your integrity. That is a completely personal decision. Take time to contemplate it. Decide how you are going to put your best foot forward without taking any personal steps back.

2. *It's Still a ~~Straight Man's~~ Metrosexual's World*. It used to be simply a straight man's world. But now, queer eyes have coerced straight men into improving their appearance. Without a doubt, the influence of gay men on fashion and physical shape is sharpening straight men at work. What's becoming clearer is that this makes it more competitive for women. If guys are dressing better and taking care of themselves, why not you?

3. *Professional Doesn't Mean Totally Asexual*. Women don't have to dress like male bankers from the 50s (i.e., a conservatively cut blue or gray suit with simple blouse) to look professional. There's a lot you can do to maintain your professional look without sacrificing your sex appeal. Focus on your best features but don't overdo. For instance, if you want to show off your legs, wear tailored skirts a little above the knee. Add color to whatever you are wearing to jazz it up.

4. *Unisex Bathrooms Are Cool; Unisex Attitudes Are Not*. The *Ally McBeal* unisex bathroom was a step forward in the battle for equality among the sexes. The way the female characters acted while they were in the bathroom was not. Too often, women feel they have to personify the male stereotypes they've experienced. You

know what I am talking about—tough-talking, compassion-free, and joyless men. Hopefully, these male stereotypes are slowly going the way of other outdated notions, such as less pay for equal work.

5. *Follow the Gays and Shake It Up!* When gay men reject the stereotype of how they should act and dress in the workplace, the dynamic changes for women. From what I've seen, gay men have less trouble with women's power in the workplace, so they are more accepting of women as colleagues, subordinates, or bosses. Hopefully, fewer conflicts and changes in attitude will mean an easier time for women in leadership roles.

6. *Embrace the Erin Brockovich Factor.* Thank God for Erin Brockovich, and for Julia Roberts bringing her wild persona to the screen. In her trashy miniskirts and hooker ensembles, Erin was a legal crusader working within a male-dominated world of lawyers and bureaucrats. She fought them every step of the way, in her leopard print bustiers, skintight leggings, and fierce pumps. When her older male boss knocked her provocative outfits, she countered with jabs at his lame ties and ill-fitting suits. Guess what? She won. Now that's the kind of workplace you can embrace!

29

YOU'RE MARRIED . . . BUT ARE YOU TURNING INTO YOUR MOTHER?

Like mother, like daughter, like hell! Once you're married, how to spot the signs you're becoming mom before it's too late.

"But I don't want to become a boring suburban housewife!" wailed my friend Lisa, a twenty-seven-year-old ex–dot commer. "Promise me you won't let me become d-d-dull!" she cried on my shoulder, an hour before her wedding on what was supposed to be the happiest day of her life. No, they weren't tears of joy, as her idiot aunt who looked like Florence Henderson thought. They were tears of panic.

What they never tell cool young women who get married with the intention of settling down and having babies is that you'll have a different kind of cold feet. The typical bride's case of cold feet is traditionally more about "Is he the right choice? Does he really love me? Do we complement each other?"

The cool girl's case of cold feet is more like you're frozen with fear at the thought of 2.5 kids, a minivan, and, worse, losing your cool girl hipness. I want to make sure you have the easy-to-follow rules for keeping your cool girl hipness, even when cruising to soccer practice in your gas-guzzling suburban assault vehicle.

So what is hip? I love Sandra Bernhard's take on it: "Hip? A joint between your ass and your stomach? I don't know. Hip doesn't really come into play anymore as far as I can tell. If you're natural and you can handle yourself in any situation and roll with the punches and basically be cool and be kind to people and not be attitudey and fucked-up and trying to be cool, then you're hip."

Maybe you grew up feeling you'd have to change your personality after "I do" and the birth of your kids and become a perfect Stepford wife. You don't. I grew up in a world where men had to be straight. They don't. Part of how you keep your hip chick attitude is that you relish your imperfections rather than pretend to be perfect.

Nowadays everyone races around; two cars, two jobs, two kids, two adults a little lost because they don't have enough time to take care of their inner selves and the things that they loved in their youth. It may seem like there's no time to be hip, but your gay best friend can empathize and help. Gay men may not be in the same boat as you, but we share similar challenges. Living with any partner can be claustrophobic, all relationships involve hard won negotiation, and careers are demanding. Add kids to the mix and you have an even greater demand on you and your partner's time and attention. So consider these options next time you feel like wailing like Lisa did, worried that dullness is encroaching:

1. *Gay Boyfriend Annual Reviews.* It's too bad that reviews happen only at work. Sure, there's an unsavory judgmental aspect to them. We are used to hearing feedback based on others' opinions of what they expect us to be. But with your gay best friend, you don't have to worry about that. What we bring is honest feedback without an agenda. "What do you want to be?" is the question. Or, more to the point as the years pass, "Who are you now?" "I know I am becoming more impatient and way more judgmental, just like my grandmother," says twenty-five-year-old Andrea. "I expect my gay friend to not let me get away with becoming stuck in my ways and attitudes like she is."

2. *Hold On to Your Voice.* There are so many voices in our heads, and they increase as we age. So how is this different from schizophrenia, you ask? It's a good question, isn't it? Women's internal voices include daughter, professional person, girlfriend, wife, mom, citizen, and, of course, the "real" person who is separate and unlimited by any of those labels. You lose the "real" person's voice if you don't watch your step. "I know my mom lost her voice. Now that I am wife and mother, I see why," says Pat, a thirty-eight-year-old new mother in Philadelphia. "The loss of identity and constant demands can be overwhelming."

3. *Schedule Grown-Up Time-Outs.* Time-outs work miracles for small children who quickly learn to understand that when Mommy says "Time out," she means business. So I am going to do the same thing to you. Sched-

ule time-outs away from work, kids, and daily hassles, just like you schedule business appointments and play dates for the kids.

4. *Make a Few Unconventional Choices.* If you've chosen a traditional life of marriage and motherhood, you are going to need to buck the traditions now and then. I am here to help. You may be mommy to the kids, but underneath I still see my fun playmate and partner in crime.

21

THE GAY MAN'S WORKOUT FOR STRAIGHT WOMEN

Lift weights now, avoid dangling arm flesh
later, and other tips from the boys who
watch you do girly aerobics at the gym.

Sweat to the oldies all you want, but if you want to walk straighter and build muscles that will aid your metabolism in losing weight and allow you to knock the socks of that bimbo who's checking out your man, get those dumbbells out now.

Listen, it might seem like there's not much you should emulate about gay male behavior at the gym. Gay men need to be reminded that the term "circuit training" applies to working out, not just planning for weekend bacchanalia. And some of us should save gossiping for a less public locale. But lifting weights is one thing you can glean from the gay gym routine.

As thirty-year-old New Yorker Jamie says, "A huge part of my life is working out and going to the gym. I'm into lifting heavy weights and being strong. I thrive on that. But I hesitate to tell other women how strong I've become (yesterday I did 90-pound lat pull downs, and one-arm dumbbell rows with 45 pounds! Not bad for a 118-pound chickie, right?). Either they think I'm showing off, they start to feel insecure, or they totally can't relate if they're not into weight training. Straight men get kind of freaked out by it. Either they're insecure and competitive ('I'm the man. I'm the strong one!'), or they think I'm not feminine enough. Thank God for gay men. They're so supportive. They love my muscles and admire the fact that I am taking good care of my upper body and not limiting my workouts to hopping up and down on the stair climber. Of course, they have some of the best bodies in my gym, so I love talking to them about workouts.

"I have started doing tricep exercises like crazy to avoid the old lady underarm dangling flesh syndrome. I don't want is to wave goodbye to my boyfriend and have not only my hand but also my arm flesh waving 'buh bye' to him."

I know that some of you have concerns about working out with weights. Some of the old fears include worries that you'll get big and bulky or that it will somehow be unfeminine. I remember a trainer telling me that women neglect their upper bodies for fear of bulking up and looking like some scary squarely built Russian gymnast they saw on TV once. You won't get bigger, you'll get stronger and get arms that will look great in more revealing clothing. Arms that are skinny aren't so cool. No man wants to hold a bag of bones. Even the modelizers are in it for the "model attitude" and status, not necessarily the thrill of slipping an arm around Heidi Klum's bony waist.

Or maybe you don't look forward to dealing with the

stereotypical blockheads who make grunting noises as if they're giving birth as they hoist barbells and walk about the weight floor as if they're gang leaders.

That certainly happened to twenty-eight-year-old Jeannie from Philadelphia. "I'll drop one thousand dollars for an annual membership at some swanky place rather than put up with the giant frat house that is a typical lame, lowbrow gym. The last gym I went to had dorks decked out in their wife-beater shirts and naked-lady tattoos. They always work out in posses, it seems. They looked like they ate people for lunch. When the grunts started coming, it was like being at a grunting contest. Oh my God, they were so proud! Then as I was waiting I had to listen to them. Their conversation went like this, with lots of 'ums' and 'duhs' factored in:

"You know what's great about this place, dude?"

"No, what, bro?"

"If you do squats right here, you can look across to where girls do those hip flex machines. You know the ones, where they open like butterflies?"

"Yeah! You know what else is great? When they do their spinning classes and start doing the jumps. Gotta dig that, bro."

"Seriously, it was like the ugly guy roadshow of *Grease*," continued Jeannie. "I expected them to start singing 'Greased Lighnin' ' right then and there. Such blockheads!"

One way to overcome this is to go where the blockheads aren't. "I started out at this boxing gym because it was near my house. Wrong move. The clientele were almost all men who'd been regulars for ten years or more. I was not only new; I was a girl and didn't fit in. It was not a good environment for a girl just getting into weightlifting. I go to a 'girly man' corporate gym and I feel like the cool chick who could take anyone of these middle-aged guys. So once I got into weights there, it wasn't so intimidating," says Carrie, a thirty-four-year-old sales representative from Chicago. "It became part of my routine."

So do as the gay guys do! Your "gay guy" card will literally be taken from you if you don't belong to and visit a gym, at least semiregularly. The gym holds a sacred place in our lives. Sure there are mental health benefits, but there's a clear surface appeal too. When we have a hard time getting to the gym, the idea of walking into a gay bar or restaurant and facing critical stares is enough to keep you pumping iron!

Cathleen decided to adopt the same attitude. "I wanted to do weight training for weight loss and I ended up joining a gym with personal trainers. Think about your exercise as something good you are doing for yourself. Sometimes it might be the only good or challenging thing that you do that day for yourself. That led me to take on weight training as a fun challenge rather than as a chore."

Based on the stories from women spotlighting the benefits they've experienced both physically and socially from weightier workouts, and of course secret training tips from gay men, here are a few of the tips you'll learn:

1. *Headline: Straight Boy Melts over Girl with Hot Delts.*
   Straight guys notice girls with buff upper bods. It isn't

just about the boobs, it's about overall tone. It's highly unlikely you'll wind up looking like a bulked up Russian gymnast. To bulk up, you have to higher levels of testosterone than most women have. So chances are that weights will tone and shape, not make you look like Shrek.

2. *An Overaerobicized Apple Just Becomes a Smaller Apple.* I work out with international fitness expert Madeline Dolente, who tells her female clients that, "If you have an apple or pear shape, just doing aerobics will only make you a smaller apple or pear. It won't make you toned and tight. Women with strength appeal to guys! With a tighter upper and lower body, you'll feel more confident and sexier in bed. He imagines tight, strong legs wrapped around him. Look at Jennifer Garner. She's not petite. She's strong, lean, and defined. That's sexy.

3. *Eating Like a Bird Is for the Birds.* Don't eat like a bird. Eat like the gay guys you see going to the gym. It used to be not that long ago that diet advice for young women was to "eat like a bird to maintain that figure!" Hello anorexia! Gay guys into fitness are careful about what they eat, but they eat. "I like the approach that my gay guy friends have to working out, building muscle and keeping metabolism high. They eat several small meals daily. It's much better than girly starvation diets," says thirty-five-year-old Suzanne from New Jersey. Madeline says, "If you eat like a bird, you'll perform like a bird. Food is fuel."

4. *Burn, Baby, Burn*. More muscle mass means your metabolism burns calories faster. Find me a straight woman who won't appreciate that! Fat looks heavier than muscle though they weigh the same. Plus, the more muscle you have, the faster your metabolism is. Thus, if your body all over has more muscle mass, the piece of cheesecake will burn quicker. Works for me. As if there weren't enough good reasons to make sure the body is toned upper and lower and middle, there's a great motivation! Strength training builds muscle and increases metabolism rate. For every pound of muscle, you have to burn about thirty-five calories a day. For every pound of fat, you have to burn about two calories.

5. *Make the Gym Your Second Home*. If you are going to be going there a lot, you need to think of the gym as your home away from home. That means you have the feel comfortable there. Be careful with your choice. Don't be intimidated by women or men who look fitter than you. Madeline's tip is, "Instead of feeling bad about yourself when you someone in awesome shape, use that to motivate you. At least you are there, striving to be your personal best."

6. *Aim for Big Shoulders Without Joan Crawford*. Everyone laughs now at the exaggerated shoulder pads that made movie star Joan look like she played defense for the New York Giants. Except for the "no wire hanger" bipolar meltdown, Joan had it right when it came to fashion. She emphasized her shoulders to minimize

other aspects of her figure. Now, of course, you have to create that look more authentically, since shoulder pads have been out since *Dynasty* left the television airwaves. It's all about building the shoulders and triceps if you want to maximize the width of your upper body in order to minimize your hips. Performing lateral raises, tricep exercises, and overhead raises will give you that "shoulder-pad worthy" look.

7. *No, a Haircut Will Not Make You Thinner.* It might give you the illusion that you are thinner. It might even frame your face in a way that maximizes good features and hides chubby cheeks. It's amazing to me the number of women's magazines that constantly advertise articles like "Haircut for a Thinner You!" That old wives' tale is right up there with biblical hero Samson losing his power after a haircut from temptress Delilah. First, Samson had a Fabio look, and apparently thought this meant he was a stud. I am sure he looked better with a shorter style. Second, tell me how losing hair somehow reduced his muscular strength. While you are at it, tell me how cutting eight ounces of hair will make you lose twenty pounds.

8. *Sssh! This Is a Big Secret: Boys Don't Like Lifting Weights Either.* No one really likes lifting weights. Okay, maybe a few people do, but a lot more don't. Do you honestly think that all those gay men at the gym are having the time of their lives pumping up their delts and triceps? No. They are thinking of the metabolism benefits and how they'll fit into the new Dolce and

Gabbana muscle shirt they just bought. It's a necessary evil for a lot of us. Don't wait until you like them before you take up them up. You'll be waiting forever, eventually with slumped shoulders and dangling arm flesh. Turn it into a daily challenge, something that you control, a goal. If you approach it like that, it becomes something that you can achieve on your own (and how rare is that these days when everything from work to family, friends, and relationships are so collaborative). Best of all, the results speak for themselves.

22

BEING SPONTANEOUS DOES NOT APPLY TO YOUR HAIR!

Why you must stop getting drastic, funky hairstyles after a bad day (or before an awards show).

"The emotional connection with hair is amazing," said twenty-seven-year-old Jennifer from Dallas. "Some days I truly believe that the world will open up to me if I get a haircut." Other days, she sinks into a foxhole of anxiety, fighting an onslaught of trichotillomania, the irresistible urge to twist and pull one's own hair.

When straight men have a bad day, they head to a bar or the couch. When straight women have a bad day, they head to the nearest beauty shop. Actually, if it's a really bad day, money is no object and they head straight to the magical hair designer of their choice. I have known women who clipped coupons for food but thought nothing of hopping a plane to New York for the miracle cure to all of their problems: a cut and blow dry from Bergdorf's salon.

I have also known women who looked flawless at

lunchtime but, after that bad business meeting and subsequent trip to the salon, looked like shaggy hobbits after a rough night in the woods. Without placing their prized manes in the hands of trusted professionals, these women were, in fact, lost in the woods.

"I had a really rotten day last year at work and, instead of doing something sensible like calling a friend, I took it out on my hair," says Mary, a thirty-two-year-old marketer in Washington, D.C. "I literally walked into a salon, signed up for the next stylist and ended up with an uneven hack job. I was just so frustrated by my day and wanted a change. Honestly, I felt so cheap afterward, like I had cheated on my regular stylist and picked up someone at a bar."

I want to point out why this knee-jerk response to a bad day often makes things worse. Look at the poor forgotten actress who played Felicity in a top-ten rated television show. She had a bad day, got her long, golden curls lopped off into a pageboy, and her show got canceled. Don't let this happen to you. I've counseled many women who've done what I now call "acting out on your hair." Heed their cautionary tales, girls! I know all too well what's at risk when you make fast and thoughtless hair changes. Gay men like me who came of age in the 80s have to mentally revisit hair horrors such as the mullet, mousse abuse, and, of course, our vain attempts at high, wild and tinted Jon Bon Jovi locks. The risks for bad hair are high: public humiliation, emotional spirals, and brittle split ends.

Most gay men are uber careful when it comes to hair maintenance. One could argue that straight men don't have to be as careful. Their peer groups don't expect as much.

Gay men cannot risk our looks due to a bad day or a momentary, fleeting whim. Nor should you. Instead, I'll give you alternatives for managing those bad days that will make you feel better but leave your hair and pride intact.

These stories will make you think twice before you chop it all off, get talked into the asymmetrical look, bleach it until the remaining strands cry out for mercy, or tease it into a skyscraper.

"I didn't know when I walked into the salon as a brunette with a pageboy style that I'd emerge two hours later with a platinum-blond punk cut," says Sarah, a thirty-four-year-old sales executive from Virginia. "It was definitely a physical manifestation of emotional change. In retrospect, I set out a big blond flare to my fiancé when things were going south between us."

Sometimes the irresistible urge for an extreme hair makeover signals emotional trouble. Maybe you are having a hard time with your boyfriend, parents, or work. Sometimes it signals a need for change due to extreme boredom. Beware boredom! Or at least, react by adopting a productive hobby. Don't take it out on your defenseless hair like thirty-year-old Lisa did to her beautiful, naturally wavy brown locks.

"I didn't realize it at the time, but I felt blasé in my personal life. I got my brown hair dyed bright blond, like Blondie. My dad paid me four hundred dollars to dye it back, so in a way I learned that I get rewarded for BHB (bad hair behavior). Another time, in my twenties, I was bored again. I went to the salon and got the 80s shaved Sinead O'Connor look, my long hair clipped to fuzz all over. My fiancé didn't even recognize me as he walked by me on the street." Looking like a Hare Krishna neither helped her boredom nor her fashion sense. Lisa's friends and husband now go out of their way to keep her occupied and interested. They live in fear of boredom striking again, yielding a new, scary hair choice.

Then there are those times when underlying emotional concern and boredom aren't the root causes of scary hair. Sometimes bad hair happens, and it's just a terrible mistake. One minute you are minding your business, looking fabulous, and next thing you know, something goes horribly awry amid the rollers, brushes, curlers, color jar, and steam irons. Maybe your stylist is hung over, has an ax to grind, or, in my friend Bonnie's case, is a foreigner with the lethal combination of charm and no command of the English language.

A few years ago, I decided to take sexy Jersey girl Bonnie, with the bounce in her walk and hair, to a new salon I'd tried earlier that week. The handsome Brazilian stylist who cut my hair did a great job, and I wanted him to do the same for Bonnie. I kept telling her, "He really listens, and you'll like him." Laughing and talking, we hopped the subway uptown to the salon. After all, what could go wrong?

The stylist gave her his big smile as he ushered her into his chair. She smiled back and thought they were having a fabulous conversation, full of laughs and connection. She told him exactly what she wanted; a chic, short, and feathered hairstyle known as "shattered glass." She'd grown her hair out just to get this style. I knew we were in trouble when I looked up from my magazine and saw her frozen face and terror-filled eyes. It turned out the muy guapo man with scissors knew not a word of English! He hadn't understood a word she'd said. With a few snips, he'd clipped and snipped like a madman, leaving her with a suburban bowl cut that looked like a cross between Forrest Gump and Mia Farrow in *Rosemary's Baby*. She was shattered all right, but not in a flattering shattered glass way, that's for sure. On the way out, she burst into tears. "Why?! This isn't shattered glass. This is old lady at the Secaucus outlet mall!" she cried. "Dave, you said he was fantastic. But you left out one small detail. He doesn't speak English!" I held her hand as we slowly walked downtown in the rain. Within an hour, we headed out again to a tried and true stylist who did her best to fix the bowl cut.

I felt awful that I mistook his mute charm for fluency in English, but didn't offer too much consoling. I focused on action. I manned the phone like we were in a war room until a "fix the disaster" appointment was set. This was an emergency.

My point is: when you have the mane equivalent of a drive-by shooting, your gay boyfriend will help you fix it. We get it. It's a bad haircut and it's the end of the world. We'll also encourage you to speak up before it's too late. Knock the scissors out of the stylist's hands if you must. Knee him in the groin before he can do more damage! Women learn self-defense for security. Now they need to apply those best practices in defense of their hair.

Suzanne, a thirty-four-year-old New Jersey native, wishes she had practiced the art of self-defense on the stylist who gave her a mullet. "I went to Elizabeth Arden with a gift certificate. I kept telling the new stylist that I didn't want a cut. But he chopped it anyway. As he cut, it was like my tongue froze. He was hell bent on giving me a bad version of The Rachel from the television show *Friends*. When he finished and made me face the mirror, I looked like Carol Brady. I hated it, but everyone kept saying, 'It's fine, it's fine.' Then my gay friend walked in, took one look at me, and sighed. 'Oh well, it'll grow back. Where are the headbands and gel?' We made a pact to measure it every week. Once it was long enough, he went with me to get a fashionable bob."

Hair is an instant way to reinvent yourself. That means it's dangerous. If you are most likely to make a change after a solid week of bad hair days, there's not a judge in the land who'd shoot down your decision. But if you're itching from a bad day and instant gratification seems too slow, stop yourself. Remember the old adage, "Don't shop when you're hungry?" Don't get a cut when you are frustrated because you're likely to have buyer's remorse. Don't race to the salon when you have PMS, when you are under duress, or after a fight with your boss or boyfriend.

"I am most likely to make an extreme hairstyle choice after a breakup," says Renee, a thirty-two-year-old hotel manager in Nashville. "I have an 'I'll show him' attitude." Last time Renee did this, the only thing she showed anyone was an oversize red-haired perm that made her look like Little Orphan Annie's mom. To minimize the curl, Renee took the advice of a woman's magazine and applied mineral oil liberally. "That only made it worse. Now I looked like the white trash version of Little Orphan Annie's mother. At that point, I was ready to pack it in, get a trailer, and go on the *Jerry Springer Show*. Where were you when I needed you, honey?"

I was too late to help her that time. Hopefully, Renee is reading this book, and can take the following advice to ward off future calamities:

1. *Plan to Be Spontaneous Tomorrow.* Don't make rush decisions when it comes to your hair. Never run from a breakup to the barber. Never give yourself a haircut after three margaritas. When it comes to your hair, be like Scarlett O'Hara and think about that tomorrow. Hopefully, by tomorrow you'll consult with your gay boyfriend before your chances for a cool hairstyle are gone with the wind.

2. *Beware the Boyfriend with a Hair Agenda.* In general, beware the boyfriend who pushes you into any kind of agenda. If he's trying to control your hair, what else is he trying to regulate in your life? Ultimately, you need to make hairstyle choices that will make you happy. As thirty-six-year-old Nina from Seattle says, "My boyfriend kept telling me to grow my hair long. Maybe it was some Crystal Gayle fantasy he had. But I look awful with long hair. It gets stringy and makes me look old. I talked it over with my gay friend Kevin, who told me to forget growing hair to my ass when I look younger and smarter with a short style." In this kind of situation, I always tell women to turn the tables. Tell him you'll agree to what he wants if he'll agree to a few of your demands, such as cleaning up after every messy dish, losing twenty pounds, and whatever else you know he'll never do.

3. *Stop the Bleaching!* Somehow, women who indulge in excessive bleaching think frizzed, fake-looking hair that's in danger of falling out quicker than Janet Jackson's boob at the Superbowl is superior to hair that highlights and flatters their features. I've never met a straight man who thought an overly bleached blonde was ideal for more than one night (and even then, in dark lighting). Blond done well is a thing of beauty. Blond done poorly is a crime against nature.

4. *Do Not Keep Your Hair as High as Your Hopes.* Julie, a twenty-nine-year-old Georgia peach, was desperate to look fabulous for her date. Twenty minutes before he was scheduled to arrive, she was in her bathroom having a "Vegas-worthy prizefight" with her hair. She ratted, twisted, teased, and used what she considered a "fancy ass" product as the clock ticked. At the end of this ordeal, her hair looked like the Eiffel Tower. It wasn't exactly Paris when it sizzles. "Sweetie, you try being a Southern woman in a modern world. It ain't easy," she told me. I am sure it isn't. But it's easier than being a bald Southern woman whose hair finally threw in the towel after years of abuse. And it's easier than having your hair vivisected by a ceiling fan. It's true that Southern women and high hair go together like fried catfish and hush puppies. I come from a Southern family and know all about skyscraper hair. The "because that's the way I've always done it" rationale is as good for you as that fried catfish. Reconditioning your mindset is just as important as conditioning your hair.

5. *The Art of Self-Defense Starts in the Stylist's Chair.*
Sadly, stories of women whose tongues were tied in the
stylist's chair are common. What happened to Bonnie
and Suzanne is happening now to women across the
country. What can women do to mount a defense
against hair stylists who chop hair like butchers chop
meat? Start with self-defense. As soon as a snip or clip
you don't like happens, speak up! Grab the scissors if
you have to, and keep an eagle eye on your hair at all
times in the chair. Beware the hair artiste who fancies
himself a modern Monet, wanting to turn you into his
piece of art. People often prey on your insecurities for
their own ego purposes or to get more money. Don't
doze off to the pleasant music, only to wake up in dire
need of three-month seclusion or a wig.

6. *It's a Hairdo, Not a Hair "Don't."* Experiment cautiously. Remember, gay guys proudly walked by your
side when you left the house with Goth hair in eighth
grade. Sometimes, we even dyed ours black to match
yours. So, don't get me wrong. I want you to experiment. It's just that now the stakes for experimentation
are higher. You can't get your mother to write you a
note keeping you out of work, like she did school,
when your home hair highlighting "chemistry experiment" goes awry. You can't get a Sinead O'Connor
total buzz cut and expect your family and friends to
think you are in your right mind. Before any major decisions, consult at least three people whose opinions
and taste you trust.

7. *Feeling Crazy? Get a Wig.* Playing dress up is one of life's great joys. Take Halloween away from me and I'd be bereft. It's the one night of the year I get to legitimately be a pirate, tasteless celebrity, or drug-addled rock star. But I also know the difference between playing dress up and getting stuck in a fashion time warp. You want to look like Courtney Love or Pink on Grammy night? Let's buy you a wig, squeeze you into ripped black fishnets and slip you into a miniskirt held together with toothpicks and barbed wire. At the end of the night, you can chuck it all and change from scary, punk Cinderella back into the girl we all love. But let's not do anything permanent, like dip your hair in pink color so that you end up looking like a reject from the movie *Grease*.

8. *Show and Tell, Don't Just Tell.* Visuals are important not only for style and length, but also for color. Nowadays, there are just too many options for women's hair color. This is something that most guys don't have to worry about, with a few exceptions such as "Mr. Overly Highlighted" and "Mr. Orange Trying to be Light Brown." If you are doing it yourself, you face a multitude of over-the-counter choices. It used to be simple, didn't it? You'd ask the bored shop clerk for light brown coverage. Now to get light brown coverage, you must choose between colors with names such as nutmeg, toasted almond, spiced cider, and gingerbread. What is this? A county fair? The shades shown on the boxes are no help. We

all know they lie. If you are relying on a color stylist, how do you verbally explain shades of color? My suggestion is to pretend like it's "show and tell" time at school and present pictures of what you want to your stylist.

23

ARE THEY REALLY TALKING BEHIND YOUR BACK?

How a gay man can tell friend from foe.

Many gay men learn at a young age to be silent but acute observers of human behavior. After all, we keep our mouths clamped about a big part of our identity until sanity and hormones kick in, helping us to come out. Then we really start living and join the party, but we retain our powers of observation. That makes gay men invaluable to you when we give you feedback about the people in your life.

It's like having your own superhero with magical X-ray vision who can see into the minds and motivations of those around him. Because I am fiercely loyal to you, you'll know if I feel someone around you is not treating you well. Part of my loyalty also includes letting you know when I think you're being overly sensitive and too harsh in your judgment of others.

There's truth in Oscar Wilde's statement, "It is perfectly

monstrous the way people go about, nowadays, saying things against one behind one's back that are absolutely and entirely true." But more likely, the things said behind your back are neither true nor objective. Usually, the people saying things behind your back have an agenda a mile long that usually furthers their goals.

I am not an advocate for you knowing exactly what people say about you when you aren't around. The healthier approach to adopt is, "What people say about you is really none of your business." Gay men know all too well how gossipy comments turn a big town into a small town in no time flat.

But when obvious agendas are at play, you need to know how to tell who's on your side. As Buddha said, "An insincere and evil friend is more to be feared than a wild beast; a wild beast may wound your body, but an evil friend will wound your mind." Here are my secrets for helping you distinguish true friends from two-faced foes:

Are the People in Your Life Friend or Foe? What Do You Need to Look Out For? Your Gay Boyfriend Tells All

GIRLFRIEND

- Beware Miss Know-It-All. Of course, no woman makes it through life without key girlfriends. They are a godsend. But beware the friend who thinks she knows what's best for you. "Even my girlfriends think that they know what's best for me. Despite the fact that there are more single people in the world than ever before, old dynamics die hard," says twenty-seven-year-old Michelle.

- Beware the judgmental girlfriend. "My friend is too rules-y. She second-guesses my every move and says things to my friends about me like 'He broke up with her because she slept with him too soon,' " says thirty-five-year-old Sarah. Friends don't judge your dating habits and ally themselves with your guy. This kind of behavior usually masks either competitiveness or anger. "After my divorce, I regretted telling a girlfriend about a new date, a friend of my ex's. I was judged really harshly," says thirty-two-year-old Dana. "Turns out she had dated him, a small fact I had to find out from someone else."

- You have a right to question her intentions if she tells you details about the terrible things someone said about you behind your back. Someone could truly have your best interests at heart when they tell you to be careful around someone who is not being kind to you. Then again, it could be a scene right out of *Mean Girls*. There are ways to make it clear someone is not supportive of you without telling you the gory details. Anyone who tells you all the details is not being considerate of your feelings.

BOYFRIEND/HUSBAND

- Beware the Staller. We all know this guy too well. When you have something important on your mind and want to discuss it, he's full of answers like, "Sure, soon, not now, but soon, OK?" When a guy continues to ignore a topic that's important to you, it's time to ignore him. Once, when I was telling a straight friend how several women I'd interviewed told me about boyfriends who'd evaded important topics, he said to me, "The problem is that people just don't take personal responsibility for what they say and do anymore, but don't quote me." Point made?

- Pay attention to checks and balances, and not just early on. In other words, make your guy earn your fabulous attention, and continue to earn it. It's easy to get caught up in the traditional girl-caretaker role, but don't unless he's taking good care of you right back.

- Don't let him define what's normal in your relationship. As your gay boyfriend, I see too many women let their guy set the tone for how they interact, cohabit, and relate.

PARENTS

- Become Miss Independent. For gay guys, coming out is often the time when we rise up and claim our independence. It often involves conflict with parents, and I don't think I've ever met a gay man who's regretted standing up for himself with his parents. It's your right to live as you wish and to expect respect.

- Step outside the subjective mother/daughter circle. Get objectivity on how your mother is responding to you. You are so used to your mother that maybe you can't tell when she's pushing her agenda that may not be in your best interest.

- Question the value of being daddy's girl. Sometimes there are hidden costs. One of them is allowing yourself to be infantilized. Many women with overly attentive and generous daddies don't know why their relationships with men are screwed up. Why aren't they fully living in the world? On the plus side, you get an unlimited American Express card. On the downside, you really don't have much of a life. Prada dress: $650. Fendi purse: $499. Daddy's princess escaping from confining daddy prison: priceless.

COWORKER

- Find at least one fabulous gay friend at the workplace. Okay, I am biased, but your gay coworker might provide unique perspective and loyalty. As twenty-seven-year-old corporate manager Angela says, "My gay coworker has my back and lets me know who's on my side. He has insight into interpersonal relationships in a way that some straight men don't, or at least don't share. Either the gay guy's emotional intelligence quotient is higher or he's just willing to share it with me more freely." In terms of loyalty, when a gay coworker shares his sexual orientation with you, it's usually a statement of trust and faith in you. After all, this is work, and you never know how people are going to react. Gay guys appreciate all the support we can get and are usually willing to return it in spades.

24

DO YOU LOOK FAT IN THAT OUTFIT?

Could the answer be yes? It's not you, it's the clothes! If your goal is "camouflage dressing," you may not be as undercover as you think.

"Do I look fat in this outfit?" is one of the all-time no-win questions. Millions of husbands and boyfriends have been reduced to pulp in an emotional Cuisinart by not answering the question quickly, honestly, or dishonestly enough.

But I will tell you the truth. Outfits aren't the only thing that makes you look fat. Fat makes you look fat. You know what else? Outfits don't make you feel fat when you don't look fat at all. Pressure from Madison Avenue to look like a beanpole makes you feel fat. Finally, the quickest and surest way to have people think you look fat in an outfit is to ask them if you do. I know I am not the first person to offer these pearls of wisdom, but someone really needs to face the concept of "camouflage dressing" with you. You shouldn't face it alone.

Camouflage dressing is the name given to the fine art of

clothing choices that hide what you feel are your most un-flattering physical traits. Black leggings and huge, oversized men's shirts are the caftans of our time. What are the myths about camouflage dressing? That it is a quick fix? That it will allow you to hide your body? You rarely cover up that part or parts of you that you're trying to hide. What you say about yourself when you dress this way says more about you than any outfit. Sometimes when you camouflage dress, the only person you are fooling is yourself.

If you want to dress thinner the right way, I offer tips from women who do it better than anyone. But remember, it doesn't work that well. So get a handle on what's really happening. Gay men know about living up to overly high expectations.

If you want to feel pressure about how you look, morph into a gay man walking into a gay bar on Friday night. The once-over look from a gay man is one of the most amazingly efficient and comprehensive physical assessments. Behind the eyes, you see the wheels turning in grand makeover fashion. He's too thin, too fat, too short, too confident, not confident enough, or too "something." Is any other group as self-critical? To manage those expectations, we learn to accent our best features and hide the flaws. Why? Because we know how visually oriented men are!

We accentuate the shoulders, find ways to slim the waist, look taller, younger, and buffer. We ask a lot of our clothes and styling aids, to be sure. Some of the tried and true "do's and don'ts" that I've seen women employ to look thinner and more stylish are:

Do

- Play to your body type strengths and weaknesses. If you are apple-shaped, then keep the focus off your stomach and hips. Avoid fitted looks that cinch in the middle.

- Lessen horizontal lines and focus on vertical lines. Jeri, a thirty-year-old manager at Club Monaco, says, "Try to look and act taller. It's the simplest thing you can do to look thinner." OK, but the image of women straining like giraffes is frightening. If "walking tall" doesn't work, go for long lines such as lean pencil skirts, stick with three-quarter-length coats worn either as an overcoat or as part of a pantsuit, and wide waistband skirts that hide the belly. As thirty-three-year-old Barbara says, "A-line is what I shoot for to minimize my big old ass." Guys do the same when they wear boots for height and loose-fitting shirts worn outside the pants. The male cast of the TV show *Friends* were experts at camouflage dressing their weight.

- Stick to black. It's always in fashion, and slimming especially if worn on trouble areas.

- Cover age-giveaway areas like the neck and hands when appropriate with scarves and gloves. Diane Keaton is the role model in this department. Her use of gloves and scarves is nothing short of brilliant.

- Add some definition to a full face with a double chin with darker turtlenecks.

- Find looks that work for you and stick with a good thing.

Don't

- Wear dangly accessories and ruffled layers. As Carol says, "I had this pink madras outfit with a lot of fabric, and I wore it out. My gay friend said, 'Carol, you are never to wear that skirt again. Entire troops of people could live in that skirt. Omar the tentmaker made that skirt.'

- Wear clothes that are too tight and accentuate the negative instead of the positive. If you are bottom heavy, stretch capri pants should be left in Capri. If you are top heavy, avoid form-fitting t-shirts that don't flatter your form.

- Go for the horizontal striped blouse that emphasizes width.

Tips that help you manage pressures better, lessen the need to camouflage, and accent the positives are great. But the real goal is for you to feel fabulous as much of the time as possible and not feel the need to hide your awesome self. Here's how:

1. *Ask Your Gay Friend for the Truth.* In the least offensive but most straightforward way possible, I'll tell you when your look isn't working. Before you go out, tell me who you want to be—professional working woman, sex vixen heading out on a date, relaxed casual girl off for a day with friends—and I will tell you if you are on the right track.

2. *Join the Fight Against Body Fascism.* You'll find many straight women and gay men who'll join the fight with you. Who says there's only one way to look? The impossible queens and razor thin "social X-rays" who run Madison Avenue have to take some of the blame. But they just reflect society. We can choose to not buy into as much as we do now. If I bought into gay mythology surrounding looks and aging, I would have moved to Siberia following my thirtieth birthday party. Gandhi said if you want to experience change, "Be the change you want to see in the world."

3. *Put the Inner Voice Back in Its Box.* You know that small inner voice that speaks up as you are dressing and says, "What makes you think you look good in that?" Tell her to shut up. That little voice erodes confidence. Without confidence, you can wear army fatigues, greenery, and a helmet, but you still won't camouflage your low self-esteem.

25

HOW TO THROW A DINNER PARTY TO PLACATE YOUR GAY FRIENDS AND TOTALLY DAZZLE YOUR STRAIGHT ONES

Tips from the gay men who keep America's tables stylish and cutting edge.

The chapter title says it all. Your dinner party goal is to dazzle your straight friends. Keep it simple. Of course, you want to placate the gay ones, but they're never satisfied anyway, so why bother? You are a busy woman. You do not have time to travel to South America with famed floral designer Robert Isabell in search of rare orchids for the centerpiece. You can't possibly get the kids to school and soccer and spend an entire semester studying napkin design. And there's no way you can pull off a dinner party in two weeks if you have to personally engage both Dean and Deluca in the fine art of colorful, unique side dishes that match your china pattern.

In a way, it's nice to have unattainable goals, isn't it? They keep you reaching for your own personal best. If you can keep them from driving you crazy, they keep you learning and curious how to do things better next time.

What are some examples of exciting recipes? How should you decide whether to cater the dinner or make it yourself? As Carrie, a thirty-eight-year-old hospital lab technician told me, "I read recipes the same way I read science fiction. I get excited, my mind races and expands, and by the conclusion, I say to myself, 'Wow, no way that's ever going to happen.' "

Fortunately, cookbooks with every variety, taste, style, regional and country cuisine, and carbohydrate count now abound. For the time conscious, many now state how long the meal should take, start to finish. Sometimes, your planning can be completely thrown off by either a hard-to-find ingredient or a recipe that sounds simple but actually takes hours to assemble. Recently, I made grilled Chilean sea bass with fresh mango mint fruit salsa for a few admittedly finicky gay friends. I could have flown to Chile and fished for the sea bass myself, given the time it took me to assemble and then chop, dice, and mix the fruit and mint required for the salsa. Not only is timing everything for the perfect dinner party, but you should always follow common sense rules, such as never serve a new dish for the first time to guests. Practice on yourself and those closest to you, including your partner or best friend (if the recipe works within reason) or your dog (if it doesn't).

The best dinner parties I ever attended were in New York at a penthouse triplex owned by a fabulous older gay friend of mine named Douglass. Of course, the Central Park views from his flower-lined terrace didn't hurt. But it was really his approach that made the dinners so special. In this casual day and age, his dinners had a refreshing air of formality. People dressed up because they knew he would. The food and wine were always delicious and flowing, but it was his approach to the mix of people that was unforgettable. Douglas mixed more than drinks. His guests were ages eight to eighty; new people he'd met that week and old friends from years ago, and a blend of uptown, downtown, and everywhere in between. More than that, when you were at his table, you never forgot he was host. His grace and interest in all guests made us rise to our best selves. Seamlessly, he drew out us out so that, by the time you left after lingering over dessert, you felt like you'd made a connection with everyone there. Fantastic food and drinks, a gorgeous setting, the right ambience, and guests are only part of the equation for success.

Never forget that your dinner party revolves around you. It's all about creating a world and having others fully immerse and share in it. Douglass's style was more formal, but that doesn't mean you need to be formal. Gay men have always been great at creating our own worlds, and this works in our favor when it comes to throwing parties. So keep that in mind as you consider these twenty tips for helping you glean the best of gay entertaining to become an enviable homosocial hostess who knows how to throw a party with that added dash of fabulosity.

Twenty Dinner Planning Party Secrets From Your Gay Boyfriend to Make You a Homosocial Hostess

1. WHO TO INVITE?
- Be like your gay friends and mix it up. One of the great things about being gay is the freedom of not having to fit in. Invite a colorful mix of old and new, young and

old, and gay and straight. Invite at least two people who will help you lead the conversation and one wild card person you've recently met and want to get to know better.

2. HOW MANY

- Six to eight is ideal for everyone to mix and mingle. As Goldilocks would say, it's not too big or too small, it's just right.

3. WHEN

- Gay dinner parties borrow a lot from gracious Mediterranean living. Both start late and are long, languorous affairs. I wouldn't start your dinner party before 8 o'clock, especially if it's a weekend. Your party is the evening's entertainment.

4. WHAT TO SERVE?

- This isn't a lab, and your guests aren't guinea pigs. Whatever you make, make sure you've tested it on your nearest and dearest first.
- Tie the food into the season, the other dishes you plan to serve, and the theme.
- Pay attention to the details. As Suzanne recalls, "The best dinner party I went to wasn't an over-the-top soiree. It was very simple and intimate at a gay friend's apartment. He served us four courses of smaller foods, like tapas he made, with specially selected wine that went with it. There were small candles everywhere to set the mood. He invited people who I knew he really wanted us to meet, and we did end up bonding with

them. Since my mother was such a bad cook, I totally overcompensate by getting too worked up about perfection. That night reminded me that entertaining doesn't have to be a frazzling amount of work, and it isn't about trying to impress. But it is about details."

5. THEME AND PARTY FAVORS

- If you are going for a theme, go for it all the way! Make it entertaining, festive, and spontaneous. Some of the best dinner parties I have ever had or attended were theme parties, focused on Halloween, July 4th, and other holidays and events. Add a touch of the unexpected and outrageous. "At the best party I ever attended, the host hired a fabulous mixologist at the bar. He had a ton of really cool liquor and kept thrusting glasses of candy colored liquid for us to try. It loosened up the group fast and gave us something fun to talk about," says Sarah. You can also consider adding small party favors for each guest that tie into the theme.

6. COUNTDOWN: THREE WEEKS TO GO

- Two weeks or more before, invite your guests by phone or mail. In this Internet-oriented world, e-mail invitations or Evites are fine for larger parties, but you want to convey that there's something more intimate and special about your dinner party.

7. COUNTDOWN: ONE WEEK TO GO

- A few days before, buy the bulk of food. You want it fresh, but you don't want to wait until the last minute.

You'll have enough last-minute emergencies without having to worry about food. To be a true homosocial hostess, splurge and get the best food and liquor you can afford.

- Evaluate the guest responses. Based on the acceptances, invite guests to fill any empty spaces at the table. At this point, always consider inviting a wild card, a new friend or someone you've recently met. I learned the value of the wild card with gay men who love a new face. Everyone does.

- Up the festive quotient? What stands out about your party? What's your theme, or what do you want to focus on? Make sure your wine, food, and accessories reflect how special you want the evening to be.

8. DAY BEFORE

- Make sure to set out everything you'll need during the party, from cocktail trays and platters to wine glasses, wine, plates, utensils, vases, wine, candles, and music. I have never had a party where I didn't have to sprint to a store for something I was missing the day before. That's to be expected. Better to race the day before than party day!

9. RIGHT BEFORE PARTY TIME

- Lights, camera, action. It's show time! That means, get the mood set. Make the lighting flattering and relaxing. When I throw a party, I usually have enough candles lit to make you think you are attending dinner in a medieval castle. Unless you have flawless, strategically designed lighting, candles are the quickest and surest bet to make the room warm, glowing, and relaxed. I am also a believer in fabulous music. You are the host, you've set the theme of the party, so make sure the music matches.

10. DURING

- Plan for latecomers and transitions. Always allow for latecomers. Make sure cocktail hour is at least 30–45 minutes long. Have the dining area set up so that you can make the transition to dinner smoothly.
- Abundanza! Always have enough of everything. Nothing succeeds like excess. People love knowing there's plenty of food and drink. After all, you all there to indulge.
- Relax so others will follow your lead. Follow the gay dinner party rules of engagement, which include bringing out each guest and setting high expectations for people trying to mix and mingle.
- Access your inner control freak, and without being overbearing, control the seating and conversation. Be like my friend Douglass and make sure every guest is engaged. By the time dinner ends, everyone should feel they know each other better than they did when they sat down.
- At some point during the dinner, stir it up a bit. No dinner should be without a little touch of raucous bacchanalia.

11. CONTINGENCIES

- Guest glitches! What if someone brings an extra guest? Don't you hate when that happens? In this day and age, people seem to be getting lax in their manners. But if it happens, what can you do? Glaring doesn't help, and remember, your chief responsibility is to make sure your guests have a great time. So if it happens, ask yourself, "Am I a good witch or a bad witch?" Everyone will be watching to see if you melt or rise above it all like Glinda. What if guests are running late? Why is it that just when the party should be starting, invariably guests call to tell you they're late, lost, or, my personal favorite, just to chat with you en route, as if you have nothing better to do? Do whatever you need to do to stay off the phones.

- One of your dishes doesn't turn out right. Make light of it. Don't serve it. Don't obsess.

CONCLUSION:
ADJUSTING TO LIFE WITH MARRIAGE, BABIES, LOVERS, AND LONG DISTANCE

I was bridesman of honor in my friend Cara's wedding. You remember Cara. She's the one from college who drank my bourbon, took my advice, and launched me as a gay boyfriend twenty years ago. Technically, I suppose I was a groomsman or usher at her ceremony. But the truth is that we didn't know how to properly name my role in her life given the rigid roles of a traditional wedding. Her soon-to-be sister-in-law was maid of honor, and I guess her husband might think of sis as his "groomsgirl," if there were such a term. But she was family, and somehow that's different. The point is that there really is no true term for a women's closest gay male friend at her wedding.

To me, that was a metaphor for how awkward and trailblazing it sometimes feels to maintain and strengthen the gay boyfriend bond when it doesn't fit neatly into social structures. You and I face challenges to our bond due to husbands and partners, babies, geographical separations, and different life paths. If a woman gets married, her husband or family would never question her ongoing closeness with a girl-friend. Often when a woman gets married, her other girl-friends might jump on the marriage and motherhood track themselves. That's not always the case for gay men and their straight female friends. Even if we both stay single and child-less, geographical separations can pull us apart. No one is wrong or at fault. But how can you maneuver life's in-evitable changes and stay close?

I hate losing girlfriends to marriage and partners (hers and mine), motherhood, and geographical separations. But now I know that we have to fight not to let the friendships slip away. There are long-standing bonds involved. "My gay friend and I have such a long history," says Linda, twenty-nine-year-old designer, echoing the sentiments of many women I interviewed. "I was the first girl he really opened up with about being gay, the first one who was really accept-ing of him, and I think we'll always have an unbreakable bond because of that. Likewise, he was the first guy I felt I could safely talk to about adult things."

All friendships go through changes. All lives go through changes. As Karen told me, "Not only did I have to get used to you being gay, which was a huge change for me, but then I had to deal with your relationships. I wondered if I'd fit into your life, too." What I thought was just me dealing with their changes was actually us dealing with each other's changes.

What needs to happen for these unique friendships to weather the storms?

MARRIAGE AND PARTNERS

When it comes to meeting the mates, it's always a question. Will I like him? Will he like me? And even if he likes me, will he feel threatened? Several women expressed to me that their bottom line for their men is, "Love me, love my gay male friend."

But I want the feelings to be organically warmer than that. From the women's point of view, she wants the two men she loves to be close, too. "James is really important to me and I want him to be important to my husband, too," says Anna.

It works both ways, of course. Some of my girlfriends said to me, "You were the relationship changer" after I became partnered. But who changes first doesn't matter when people of like minds are willing to work at their friendship. It just takes a wide berth of patience.

"My husband was initially a little threatened by my friendship with David," says Carol. "He had lesbian friends in college but hadn't been good friends with a gay man. My relationship with David predated my husband so there was much history. With time, they struck up a friendship on their own. I'd be hard pressed to know exactly how," she laughs. "But I do know it involved electronics and basketball. It was David who often came to my husband's defense and explained to me why things were a certain way." In my research, a common theme was women who valued their gay male friend's ongoing male counterpoint. It helps bridge the communication gaps.

Another recurrent theme was how important it is to keep partners, yours and his, in the loop, even if the primary friendship remains between the two of you. Men can be curious and little bit jealous of the gay friend. Satisfy the curiosity by making sure they you all get together occasionally.

BABIES

Nowadays, it could be the gay guys who are parents and the straight friend or couple who are childless. More often than not, chances are that the babies will belong to the straight people. If that's the case, there are advantages for everyone, including the kids.

For gay men without children of our own, we get to be involved in a child's life. For many of us, gayness was an obstacle during childhood. It might have prevented us from feeling truly comfortable in our nuclear families. This might be the first time we've experienced a happy, loving family.

While it's true that gays can have the parenting experiences if we want to, it's still much harder for myriad reasons, ranging from adoption costs to legal hurdles. Sometimes our straight friends like sharing their kids with us to counter what they feel might be our missed opportunity. "My only sorrow is that my gay friend would have been such a great father," says Carol.

"My husband's best friend is gay. When we had kids, we made him the godfather of our daughter," says Suzanne. "We want her to have people with perspectives and struggles different than her mostly straight relatives. Also, our friend is single and probably will not have kids, so we thought this was a chance for him to experience children. Our brothers are married with kids and will already have that experience."

For any friends dealing with the "great kid divide"—that is, those with and those without—there are adjustments. "It's important to not let kids dominate," says Suzanne, mother of three. "The dirty little secret that people don't talk about is that marriage and kids aren't that fun sometimes. This is especially true these days when parents seem just beholden to do everything on their kids' terms. It definitely spoils the kids. But it also doesn't help you. You need an outlet that's just for you. My gay friend applauds me more than anyone and I want to keep that. He's also very protective of me and that's such a nice thing to have in my life. We have to be flexible with each other due to different lifestyles, but it's so worth it."

GEOGRAPHICAL SEPARATIONS

The idea of being separated from a truly close friend is so painful; how do you handle it when life, love, or work requires you to move?

Sometimes it's so hard to say goodbye to someone so close, you just try to avoid it. "David and I almost lost each other over a geographical separation," says Carol. "I was moving and could not deal with the prospect of saying goodbye. So I disappeared. I couldn't say goodbye. We ended up having a fight at a bar and argued down the street. I was already missing what we called our *Cosmopolitan Magazine* brunches more than anything. We'd just put out good china, open champagne, make wonderful hors d'oeuvres, and enjoy the kind of spontaneous parties where time stood still. We'd listen to music and, of course, take the *Cosmo Magazine* Quiz." David and Carol might not see each other as much as they once did, but they still speak at least once a day. "Now our relationship is so stable and core, I don't ever question his motivations on anything he's said to me. I love him unquestioningly."

Or you just spend time in a train, plane, or car to stay close. One good gay stereotype may aid and abet your staying close despite the miles. Chances are your gay friends love to travel and don't see visiting as an issue. Depending on how freewheeling you are, and which of you is more bogged down at any given time, there'll have to be compromise.

"I live in two places, New York and Connecticut," says Marla. "My husband and I both work in the city but want to have a place in the country where the kids can be freer than they are all week. That means I have to worry about family, work, bills, laundry, dogs, schools, schedules, and the list goes on. But my gay friend and I have one sacrosanct weekend once a year. We go away together, and just immerse in our friendship and ourselves. It is just one little weekend, but we both look forward to it so much during the year that it sustains us. It's almost like that play 'Same Time Next Year' but with a straight woman and gay man."

DIFFERENT PATHS

What happens if you find yourselves on completely different paths? He adopts two kids with his partner and you remain a single girl in New York? Or, you get married and settle down, yet he stays immersed in the party scene as if it's a Studio 54 version of the film *Groundhog Day*, where the glitter, lights, Liza, Halston, and hotties appear nightly?

"I get jealous of my gay friends sometimes," says Suzanne. "My gay friend Tom and his partner Dave have a great apartment, dual incomes, and travel a lot. In fact, for Tom's fortieth birthday party they went to Prague for a few days of sightseeing and fun dinners. They invited friends including my husband and me, but we couldn't go. We have three kids and it's not in the cards for us right now." Suzanne wouldn't change her life, her marriage, or her kids for a trip to Prague, but it sounds like fun. On the other hand, gay guys sometimes miss out on the joys of kids, easy and assured integration into society at large, life without prejudice, and—oh yes, I forgot—basic legal rights that Suzanne and her husband take for granted. But despite the difference in lifestyle, they keep their friendship strong because it's important to both of them.

"I went to see my friend Karen," says Michael, a thirty-three-year-old architect. "She lives in the suburbs of New York now with her two kids, three dogs, and hectic life. I think we got maybe fifteen minutes of uninterrupted talk the whole day. I felt bad that she has to hyper-task every single day. It wasn't a very satisfying visit and we both knew it. But what could we do? On the way to the train, I told her I loved her, understood her situation, and held our future wonderful times in trust until they could return. Until then, we'll do the best we can. I felt it was important to finally say something so the awkwardness didn't sink the ship."

Despite the different paths, we need each other. Core bonds of friendship trump any trivialities or stereotypes.

At the end of the day, getting older often means that your circle of friends shrinks. Everyone gets busier with lives, careers, families and friends. Keeping your true friends close becomes even more important. There's no substitute for your friends. Sharing common interests doesn't ensure close friendship. For example, raising kids the same age will not make you best friends with your neighbors. That makes as much sense as saying that all single gay men are friends. Forcing closeness is unsatisfying when there's no real connection.

"It's work to keep it together, but it's worth it. It just takes compromise. I was seeing other straight couples because I figured we'd just have more in common, but mostly we had our kids as the bond. I missed my real friends, I called my gay best friend, and he felt the same. So we set out to work harder," says thirty-two-year-old Julie.

Finally, gay men need the support from the women in their lives as much as you need us. Women can be natural cheerleaders and supporters, something that men often aren't with each other. Men, straight or gay, are competitive with each other. It's essential to have supportive women who encourage us and support our goals and lives in ways that some other friends don't. As my fabulous and wise twenty-one-year-old niece Amy says, "It's important to have women bringing you back to earth because sometimes gay men get too immersed in an often obsessively shallow world." Out of the mouths of babes!

Despite the challenges, we are forever allies, you and I. Behind every fabulous friendship are two people who need to stick together through thick and thin, preferably staying thick while staying thin.

EPILOGUE

Not only are you *great*, you really are fabulous. If you didn't know this before, hopefully you know it now. My hope is that this advice, accompanied by the many smart strategies shared by the women in this book, entertains and informs you with wit and style. My hope is that you turn the final page feeling even more fabulous, hopeful, and inspired.

Whenever you are feeling down or confused, just remember that you are not alone. Chances are that there are other women going through similar situations, with similar feelings. I know that you want to hear the straight truth about those areas of life that matter most to you: dating, men, home, family, work, style, and weight, to name a few. It's hard to get this straight truth sometimes, isn't it? Whether you can put your finger on the reasons why, don't you instinctively know the limitations and drawbacks of advice from certain sources: husbands, boyfriend, girlfriends, other family members, and yes, even nationally renowned talk show hosts? (Though he can be very effective, not every woman wants Dr. Phil yelling at her all the time. It's a no-brainer that he'll tell you to "get real" if you admit you're dating a loser. But can you imagine asking Dr. Phil for his advice on what to wear? I can see the veins popping on his neck now.)

Just remember where you can get this straight truth. Hopefully you have a gay best friend of your own who gives you the objective and compassionate advice you deserve. If not, you have this book, and me.

The stories and advice in this book are full of wisdom from women I have known for over twenty years. Maybe reading about what they've gone through will save you time and anxiety when faced with the same situations. Whether it's fixing the fatal dating flaw that's ruining your love life, understanding the mysteries of the male mind better, or plugging into gay style for your next dinner party, there's a way to make it better.

After all, don't all of us need straight talk to make ourselves more aware, confident, and strong? I know I do. The fabulous women in my life could definitely write a book about how they've helped me. Now it's my chance to return the favor!

I hope you'll visit me at my website: www.davesingleton.net. I'll make sure to keep it full of the latest tips and stories from straight women and gay men. Through good times and bad, let's stick together!

ABOUT THE AUTHOR

Dave Singleton is the author of *The Mandates, 25 Real Rules for Successful Gay Dating*, a laugh-out-loud but completely true set of rules about the making (or breaking) of men's romantic relationships. He is a weekly columnist for Match.com and the author of numerous articles on topics including relationships, pop culture, politics, and entertainment. He has worked as a marketer and promoter within the publishing industry for fifteen years for publishing houses including Hearst Magazines, Scholastic, and Time Warner.

A former resident of New York City for eleven years, Dave now lives in Washington, D.C.